GREAT EVENTS
IN THE LIFE OF
BEETHOVEN

★ *Is becoming noticeably deaf,*
1798-1801

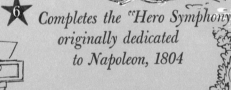

6 *Completes the "Hero Symphony,*
originally dedicated
to Napoleon, 1804

★ *Takes charge of his*
brother's son, Karl, 1815

7 *Witnesses the failure*
of his only opera, "Fidelio,"
later to be successfully revised, 1805

THE STORY OF
Beethoven

He looked neither to the right nor to the left

THE STORY OF
Beethoven

By HELEN L. KAUFMANN

Illustrated by FRITZ KREDEL

ENID LAMONTE MEADOWCROFT
Supervising Editor

PUBLISHERS Grosset & Dunlap NEW YORK

To the boys and girls who have asked me
to "do Beethoven next" this book is affectionately
dedicated

PRINTED IN THE UNITED STATES OF AMERICA
Library of Congress Catalog Card No. 57-10103

Contents

[v]

Contents

Illustrations

THE STORY OF
Beethoven

CHAPTER ONE

Two Ludwigs

W AH-WAH-WAH-H!"

The thin cry of a newborn baby came through the closed shutters of the Beethovens' house at No. 20 Bonngasse. It was snowing hard, and all other sounds were muffled, so the cry could be heard distinctly. The good neighbors on the Bonngasse nodded wisely.

"The Beethoven baby has come," they said.

In the little German town of Bonn, good news traveled fast. Grandfather Ludwig van Beethoven hurried over at once from his house across the street. He climbed the narrow stairs of the narrow house to the narrow room where Maria Magdalena Beethoven lay in bed. From within a red shawl beside her came again the cry: "Wah-wah-wah-h!"

"It's another boy, Grandfather," said Maria. "The doctor has just left." She turned back the shawl so that Ludwig could see his grandson.

"This will make up for the boy Ludwig you lost last year," he said gently. He bent down and kissed his new grandson. The baby stopped crying.

"I would like to call this one Ludwig too, Grandfather," Maria said, "if Johann is willing."

"Johann—where *is* Johann?" asked Grandfather, a trifle impatiently. His son never seemed to be where he was needed.

"Br-r-r, it's cold in here," the old man said with a shiver. "I'll go make a fire in the kitchen."

He pulled the coverlet over Maria's shoulders before going downstairs. She heard him call from the kitchen, "There's no wood here. I'll go get some. You must have a fire."

He went across the narrow street to his own house and hurried back with an armful of wood. Soon the fire in the kitchen stove blazed merrily. He pumped water from the hand pump in the garden, set the kettle on the stove, and brought Maria a cup of hot tea. She drank it gratefully.

"Where *is* Johann?" asked Grandfather a

second time, as he took the empty cup. "He should be here with you."

"He said he had a choir rehearsal," replied Maria. "He went to the Elector's palace."

"Hasn't he been gone a long time?" asked Grandfather.

"Well," said Maria, "he doesn't always come straight home from rehearsal."

Grandfather Ludwig knew this as well as she did. Both he and his son Johann were singers. He had a deep bass voice. Johann sang tenor. They both sang in the chapel of the Elector who ruled Bonn. Almost everyone in Bonn worked for the Elector. Grandfather had prospered, and people respected him, but his son was lazy.

"I hope little Ludwig will grow up to be like you, Grandfather," said Maria.

She never complained about her tall, handsome husband, but she did wish he were steadier and more serious.

"Go to sleep, Maria," said Grandfather. "I'll wait here until Johann comes. You rest while the baby is quiet."

Maria turned thankfully on her side. Grandfather sat down in the only chair.

"I will have to help bring up my grandson, that is certain," he thought grimly. "Where

[6]

is Johann? Has he gone to the tavern, as usual? Has he gone for a walk in the snow?"

Grandfather knew that the townspeople called his son Johann the Walker, for he loved to go striding over the countryside. He loved anything better than work!

At last! There was the sound of boots being stamped to shake off snow, then of footsteps on the stairs. Johann came in, whistling.

"So! *Now* you come!" said Grandfather.

"I hear I have a son," replied Johann lightly.

He went over to the bed, took off his cap, and shook the snow on Maria's face. She woke with a cry. "Johann!" she exclaimed happily. "You are here! Look what the stork brought us this time. Another boy!"

Johann poked at the baby with his finger.

"He's ugly," he complained. "Did you ever see so much hair on a new baby?" And indeed, a fuzz of black hair above a puckered little red face was all there was to be seen.

"Shall we call him Ludwig?" asked Maria.

"If you like," replied Johann. "Every Beethoven family must have its Ludwig, eh, Father?"

"He'll be my godson then," Grandfather told Johann.

[7]

"And you'll go with me tomorrow to the church to have him christened, Father?"

"Of course," replied the old man.

December 17, 1770, was a bitter cold day. In the stone church of St. Remigius, there was ice in the baptismal font. No wonder the baby cried at the top of his lungs when his warm swaddling clothes were lifted from his face, and drops of cold water were sprinkled on his forehead. He was given the name, "Ludwig van Beethoven." This means "Ludwig of the Beet Fields."

Grandfather carried his squalling godson tenderly home from the church and laid him in his mother's arms. Johann went gaily off to a christening feast at his neighbor's house.

Ludwig was a sturdy baby. He grew fast. Soon he could toddle. Then Grandfather would come over right after breakfast in the mornings to get him.

When the weather was bad, he played indoors, in Grandfather's house. It was much nicer than his own. There were thick, soft carpets on the floors. Oil paintings gave color to the walls. Grandfather gave him a silver napkin ring to roll on the carpet.

Grandfather played little tunes for him on the piano, and sang folk songs about Flanders, in Belgium, where he had lived before coming to Bonn. Sometimes Grandfather took little Ludwig on his lap, and let him strike the piano keys with his baby fingers.

On fair days, they went walking together in the streets of Bonn. The bright-eyed, lively man in the long red coat took long steps. The stubby little boy in skirts who was holding his hand had to trot fast to keep up with him. Sometimes they went down to the bank of the river Rhine, and watched the cable ferryboat go back and forth from one bank to the other. They would count the barges and sailboats carrying passengers and cargo up and down the winding stream.

Often they went to the semicircular market in the center of the town, and came home bringing black bread and purple grapes and fresh eggs and milk. But best of all little Ludwig loved the walks beyond the crumbling wall that surrounded the town. That way lay the open fields, where the grass tickled his bare legs, and the woods, where the trees arched high and made a great silence, broken only by the singing of the birds and the rushing waters of the brook.

Maria was content to see them so much together. Every morning and evening, when

On fair days they went walking together

her son lisped his prayers at her knee, she reminded him, "Pray that you will be like Grandfather."

But when Ludwig was only three, a sad thing happened. All of a sudden, Grandfather stopped coming.

"Where is Grandfather?" Ludwig asked each morning.

"Grandfather is sick in bed. He cannot come," his mother told him.

Then one day he saw Maria crying.

"Grandfather is dead," sobbed Maria, wiping her eyes on the corner of her apron. Little Ludwig did not know what it meant to be dead. But because his mother cried, he cried too.

Now there were no more long walks, no more songs and stories. The shutters on Grandfather's house across the street stayed tight shut. Johann sold all the lovely paintings and silver and furniture. But Grandfather's piano and violin and his music, and the painting of Grandfather himself, Maria kept for Ludwig. On Grandfather's name-day, she always hung a wreath of laurel on his picture. Ludwig helped her. It was his name-day, too. He always kept the picture, and he never forgot Grandfather.

[11]

CHAPTER TWO

Ludwig's First Lessons

MAMMA, Mamma, hide me! Papa's coming!"

Little Ludwig ran to his mother where she sat under the oil lamp in the kitchen, peeling potatoes. He hid his face in her apron, among the wet potato peels. Maria sighed as she laid down her knife. Tenderly she stroked the tousled black head burrowing into her lap.

"Do you hear Papa?" asked Ludwig, trembling. "Do you?"

"Be still. Let me listen," whispered his mother. Her soothing hands were rough and toil-worn, but to five-year-old Ludwig they felt soft and tender. In their touch he found comfort. And he had need of comfort, for Father Johann treated him badly.

Sometimes Johann stopped at the tavern up the street before coming home. At such times, it was best to keep out of his way. But there was not much room to hide in the kitchen, bedroom, and slant-roofed attic of the Beethoven home.

"Better go to bed, Ludwig," whispered Maria. "I'll bring you your supper later."

Thankfully, the little boy climbed the steep stairs to his trundle bed. He was not a coward. But he could not help wanting to hide when Johann came to drag him out of bed in the middle of the night, to give him a piano lesson. He sometimes wondered if Johann had started to teach him on the very day he was born. He could not remember the time when his tall father was not standing over him, making him play the piano or the violin. Whatever he did, Johann yelled at him and spanked him.

Grandfather had been so gentle. But two years had passed since Grandfather's death. Ludwig wished with all his heart that Grandfather would come to life again.

Maria did her best to protect her eldest son. But she had so much to do! There was a baby brother, Kaspar Anton Karl, in Ludwig's old cradle. There would be another baby soon. And Johann did not give her enough money to pay the bills.

Ludwig never saw his mother smile. Often he saw her wipe away the tears when she thought no one was watching. He wished he could be the one to make her smile, for he loved her better than anyone in the world.

Now he cowered under his thin blanket, listening. He heard the door slam, heard his father's loud voice: "I'm home, Maria!" Then, "Where's the boy?"

Maria answered in such low tones that he could not hear what she said.

"I'll give him his lesson late tonight, when I get home," said Johann. "Is supper ready? I have a rehearsal right after."

"Sit down and eat," said Maria. "Let the boy sleep. He's a growing boy. He needs his sleep."

Ludwig's keen ears heard the scrape of a chair being drawn to the table, and the clatter of spoon on dish. Then his father answered crossly, "Your precious son may need sleep, but I need money. Ludwig can make a lot with his music. That Wolfgang Mozart isn't the only one. Our Ludwig will be as good or better. The Mozart child made people listen to him when he was six. But now he is nineteen, not a child wonder any more. So much the better for Ludwig!"

Maria did not answer. She intended that Ludwig should go to school, even if he was to become a musician like his father and grandfather. But it was no use to argue with Johann when he was like this. And besides, it was true that Ludwig played well for a child of five. She ladled Johann's second bowl of soup in silence.

As soon as the door closed behind her husband, she carried a bowl to Ludwig.

"Take your soup while it is hot, my son," she said. "And then go right to sleep. Papa wants to give you a lesson later."

At this, Ludwig pushed away the bowl. He was hungry. But he could not swallow when he thought of the lesson to come.

"I'll say my prayers now," he said. Then, turning on his side, he closed his eyes. She kissed him good night.

It seemed only a minute later that he heard Johann stamp into the house, singing at the top of his lungs. But it was after midnight. With a clatter, Johann dragged out the footstool on which little Ludwig had to stand to reach the piano keys.

"Wake up, Schlafkopf (Sleepyhead),"

[15]

called Johann hoarsely. The boy did not answer. "It's time for your lesson," Johann called. Still no answer. Johann climbed the stairs two steps at a time. He dragged Ludwig roughly out of bed.

Oh, how sleepy Ludwig was! He rubbed his eyes and yawned and stretched. He shivered with cold. But he forced his short legs to carry him down the stairs, and up on the stool. Johann was right behind him.

"Begin!" he ordered.

Ludwig started to play. Oh dear, that chord was wrong. Through the haze of sleep, he heard that it was wrong. Smack! His father's ruler came heavily down on his hand.

"Wrong! Start again!" he roared.

Whimpering, Ludwig started again. This time, afraid he would make another mistake, he played too slowly.

"Dummkopf! Wrong tempo. I showed you yesterday. Can't you remember?" Down came the ruler again. By the time Johann said, "Genug (Enough)," Ludwig's tender knuckles were cut and raw, and he was crying.

After such a lesson, most boys would hate music. But Ludwig loved it, in spite of everything. He enjoyed the sounds he brought forth. And he listened to the other sounds that came into his mind while he played. Soon he started to make up little tunes of his own and sang them softly to himself.

One afternoon, Maria had gone to the store. The baby was asleep. Ludwig thought he was alone in the house. He tried one of his tunes on the piano. He made up chords to go with it. Johann came tiptoeing into the room. Suddenly Ludwig heard his father's angry voice. He jumped up in fright.

"What in the world are you doing, Ludwig?" cried Johann. "Stop that drumming at once, and practice your lesson."

Ludwig obediently stopped. But as soon as

[*17*]

Johann had gone out, he played his own tunes again.

Johann heard him making his own tunes on the violin too. He caught him by the ear. "What's all this nonsense you're scratching again?" he roared. "You there, scratch according to the notes, or I'll give you a box on the ear!"

"Please listen, Papa," pleaded Ludwig. "I like it, don't you?"

Johann was a musician. He knew perfectly well that Ludwig's "scratching" and "drumming" were good. But he believed that praise was bad for children. So he only said, in a somewhat softer tone:

"That's something else again. You aren't ready yet to make your own music, Ludwig. Work hard on the piano and the violin, take hold of the notes, that is what you must do. You will get ahead faster that way. When you are that far, then you can work with your mind."

Johann spoke almost kindly. It was too bad that Ludwig could not hear him later when he joined his merry friends at the tavern. There he boasted loudly:

"My son Ludwig is my only joy! Only five years old, yet he improves so in music and

[*18*]

composition that he's a marvel. My Ludwig, my Ludwig! A toast to my Ludwig!"

There was a great clinking of glasses and a hum of congratulations.

"My son will become a great man in the world," predicted Johann. "Those of you who are gathered here, and who live so long, will remember my words."

CHAPTER THREE
The Bells

BEFORE Ludwig was six, the Beethovens found their home too small for the growing family. They moved to a larger house close to the white palace of the Elector who ruled Bonn. Here the lazy Johann did not have far to go when he had to sing in the Elector's chapel. It was practically next door.

Ludwig loved the new house. He could watch the fine carriages drive along the avenue of flowering chestnut trees to the Elector's palace. He could watch the hand-kissing that went on, when the noble lords and ladies in red and gold silks and velvets came to see a play in the Elector's theater, or to hear a concert in the Elector's palace, or to worship in the Elector's chapel. On feast days, he could watch the church processions, followed

[20]

by peasants in bright, woolen Sunday-best clothes.

He loved being near the chimes in the Elector's chapel. At daybreak every morning he was awakened by their cheery clangor. They played a melody, the same one every day.

"It is from the overture to *The Deserter,* a French opera by Monsigny," Johann told him.

The chimes were so close that they seemed to be in Ludwig's room. He could feel the air vibrate around his bed when they played, and he could feel himself vibrate with them.

"The bells are my friends," he told his mother gravely. He had no other friends.

For some months, Ludwig enjoyed his friends' good-morning greeting every day. Then a terrible thing happened. In the middle of a cold January night, he was awakened by a sound like thunder. Only it was louder than any thunderclap he had ever heard. The whole house shook. Frightened, he sat up in bed.

"Mother!" he called.

Maria came hurrying in.

"Quick, Ludwig!" she cried. "Put on your coat over your nightgown. There has been an explosion. The Elector's palace is on fire. Papa is taking Karl and little Johann. You come with me."

He was wide awake now, and very frightened. He could see the red glare of the fire through the window. He took his mother's hand. Together they climbed to the roof of their house.

What a sight they saw! Flames were shooting up to the sky. The air was black with smoke. The streets were full of people. A few were helping to carry out paintings and small objects from the palace. But most stood still and watched. There was a stir when the Elector, in his nightshirt, with his nightcap tassels bobbing wildly, dashed out to safety. He had just awakened, and had not had time to dress.

It was a windy night. The flames spread from house to house. Now the whole town was awake. People were terrified. The men tried to put out the fires. But there were no fire engines, and they could not pump water into pails fast enough, nor had they enough pails. Ludwig wished he could help. But what could a boy of six do? He could only watch the fearful, beautiful flames.

At sunrise, the bells in the tower pealed forth their melody. It was a comforting sound.

"Those are my friends!" said Ludwig, squeezing his mother's hand.

But even as he spoke, the tower toppled. The flames had licked out until they reached the highest places. The tower fell to the ground with a crash. The bells fell with it. They jangled loudly, terribly out of tune, as they struck the earth.

Ludwig put both hands over his ears and cried out with pain. Ugly sounds hurt him as much as beautiful sounds pleased him, but his little hands could not shut out the sound of those jangling chimes.

He never forgot the discord of those bells that hurt his ears so. Neither did he forget the melody that he had loved, from the overture to *The Deserter*. Many years later, he wrote it into one of his pieces. And when his music told of pain or sorrow, he wrote the discords into it too.

Many houses in Bonn caught fire. The fires burned for five days. Maria was worried about the safety of her family.

"We will move," said Johann, always ready for some new excitement. "We will go back to the Fischer house on the Rheingasse." He laughed. "We'll be better off there. There's enough water in the river Rhine to put out all the fires in Germany."

Ludwig missed his friends, the bells, but he liked being near the river. He liked to lie on the bench in the kitchen by the window, and watch the huge ferryboats going from one bank to the other. Sometimes he would turn the latch of the shutter, and try to sing the squeaking sound it made. Sometimes he just lay and looked at the Seven Mountains that watched over the town of Bonn.

He was lying like this one day when Frau Fischer, their landlord's wife, came by. She was a busybody.

"What are you doing?" she asked Ludwig.

He was thinking very hard at that moment. He paid no attention to her.

"What are you looking at, Ludwig?" she asked again.

Again he did not answer. She thought he was being very rude.

"Well, I must say!" she exclaimed. "No answer is also an answer!"

Now at last he noticed her.

"Frau Fischer!" he exclaimed. "I—I was busy with such a big, beautiful thought. I didn't hear you."

"Humph!" said Frau Fischer. She went in to her house, next door, and said to her husband, "That Ludwig Beethoven is a queer one. He ought to be in school, not dreaming by the window."

Ludwig did go to school the next year. But school never stopped him from dreaming by the window and thinking the big, beautiful thoughts that he would someday put into big, beautiful music.

CHAPTER FOUR

Surprise!

ONE day in February, 1778, Maria sat crocheting a baby's sweater in the pale afternoon sunshine which came through the kitchen window. Johann stamped into the room, his handsome face ruddy with the cold.

"Catch!" he called gaily.

He tossed off his cloak, rumpled her hair, and threw a handful of money into her apron. Quietly she gathered up the clinking coins. They were his week's earnings, hardly enough to feed the family for the week to come.

"Maria, I've made up my mind," said Johann, striding up and down the little kitchen.

"To what?" she asked anxiously.

"Ludwig is eight," he said.

"I know," she replied.

"The time has come for him to make some money with his music," said Johann.

"We could use it," she sighed, thinking of unpaid bills and hungry children.

"You know, Maria, I have had very good reasons for keeping the boy at his music. I intend to make another Mozart of him. He too can be a wonder child. What those Mozarts can do, we Beethovens can do better. I intend to take Ludwig on a concert tour next month."

"Have you told Ludwig? What did he say?" asked Maria.

"You can tell him," said Johann carelessly. "It makes no difference to me what he says; he'll do what I tell him to."

"But he is only eight. Will you take him out of school?" objected Maria.

"The Mozart child never went to school at all," retorted Johann. "And I intend to say that Ludwig is six. The younger he is, the more of a boy wonder he will appear. You know that as well as I do, Maria. I'll take him to Cologne first. That is not far. He will give a concert there. If he makes money, we will go farther, like the Mozart father and son."

"But—" said Maria.

"No buts." Johann took up the poker and

rattled it on the stove-lid to emphasize his words. "You will have to make him a proper suit of clothes, Maria," he continued. "A brocade coat, satin breeches, white shirt with ruffles. That is for you to arrange. I will get him ready to play the piano. You must make him handsome."

"That will not be easy," sighed Maria, thinking of Ludwig's heavy body, short legs, and dark skin.

"Do your best," said Johann, smiling at his own handsome reflection in the cracked mirror. "It's not my fault that he's homely."

When Johann had gone out again, Maria went to the door.

"Ludwig!" she called.

She looked up and down the narrow street, shading her eyes with her hand from the afternoon sun. At the farther end, she saw Ludwig. He was riding pick-a-back on his schoolmate, Fritz Fischer, laughing and shouting. He waved his arms so wildly as he urged on his steed that he fell off. He struck the black lava pavement and rolled over into the muddy ditch at the side.

"Ludwig!" his mother cried in alarm. "Are you hurt?"

He picked himself up and ran to her, still

laughing. His face was streaked with dirt. His shirt was brown with mud, his coat sleeve was split, and his trousers were ripped.

"Just look at your clothes!" his mother scolded.

"I don't care about clothes." Ludwig muttered, trying to brush himself off.

"Come inside." said his mother. "I want to take your measure for a new suit. I have a surprise for you, Ludwig. You are going to take a trip."

"A trip! Are you going too?" he asked.

"Not this time," replied his mother. "Papa

will go with you, to Cologne. It's not far. Papa says you are to play a concert there."

She watched his face cloud.

"I am not good enough yet," he said slowly.

"Papa says you are," his mother told him firmly. "He knows. He says that I am to make you a new suit for the concert. You really will have to learn to keep yourself looking neat, my son."

She handed him soap and a towel. "Go to the pump and scrub yourself," she said. "And mind you come right back."

Ludwig went slowly, dragging his feet. His mother waited for him with her yardstick. When he came back, she preached while she measured him.

"You must look right and act right at this concert, even if you are a little boy," she said. "Remember to bow low at the beginning and end of the program, and before each piece. Make a specially deep bow to the highest nobles. If people give you presents, say, 'Thank you,' even if you don't like what they give. Don't speak unless you are spoken to. Be a nice, polite little boy."

"I'm every bit as good as those lords and ladies," said Ludwig stoutly. "Why do I have to bow to them?"

"Oh, Ludwig, wherever do you get such ideas?" asked his mother. "Stand still. I've almost finished."

It was hard for Ludwig to stand still. The boys kept calling, "Spangy, come on out." They called him Spangy, short for Spaniard in German, because his skin was as dark as a Spaniard's.

"You may go," said Maria, when it seemed he could not stand still a single minute more. When he went, however, it was not to play with the boys. He went soberly to practice the piano.

It took all the money Johann had thrown into Maria's apron to get Ludwig's outfit together. And Maria had to pawn her winter coat besides. But what an outfit it was!

She made him a sea-green tailcoat, a flowered satin waistcoat, and green satin knee breeches with buckles. She bought him white silk stockings, black shoes with rosettes, a crush hat to carry under his arm, and a gold dagger to hang at his belt. To top it all, there was a curly wig with a pigtail.

But even the fine clothes could not make Ludwig into a handsome little boy. His short body looked broader in the coat, his short legs heavier in white stockings, and his skin darker than ever under the powdered white wig. Still, when his mother helped him to try everything on, and told him how nice he looked, he began to feel pleasantly excited. In these clothes, he felt like a boy wonder. Perhaps he would play like one!

CHAPTER FIVE

The First Concert

I T WAS a blustery day in March when Ludwig kissed his mother good-by. He felt a little sad at leaving her. But what boy could be sad for long when he was going away on his first trip?

The sun was rising when Ludwig and Johann climbed aboard the sailboat that was to take them the ten miles to Cologne. They would have two or three wonderful hours on the water.

While Johann chatted with the captain, who waited for a wind to fill his sails, Ludwig sat on the hard cross-seat and looked about him. In the distance, against the sky, the Seven Mountains watched over Bonn. Its rocky cliffs and vine-clad hills, its walnut trees and fruit orchards seemed to be saying, "Come back soon."

Then the wind came up, and the boat moved out from the shore. Ludwig spied a castle. "Look!" he called to his father, pointing.

"That's the Drachenfels, the Dragon's Rock," said Johann, sitting down on the cross-seat beside him. "And over there is the Siegburg. Watch out! The sail is swinging over." Ludwig bent down clumsily. He thought the boat ride was fun. But he was getting hungry.

"When do we eat?" he asked.

"Here, I almost forgot," said Johann. "Mamma gave us some bread."

Ludwig munched his piece contentedly. The river was choppy and the boat rocked, but he was not seasick. Still, he felt a little

sick when he heard Johann untruthfully telling the captain that his wonderful son, only six years old, would play a concert in Cologne that evening.

"I'm eight years old—not six," he thought resentfully.

"All ashore!" called the captain at last. They had arrived in Cologne. They climbed out and stretched their cramped legs.

"We'll find a man with a wheelbarrow to take our box to the inn," said Johann.

Ludwig followed his father and the wheelbarrow to the inn. The street was too narrow for them to go two abreast, and it was muddy and smelly besides. The houses were small and close together. Still, the mighty spire of the cathedral towered above them, and that

was very beautiful. But Ludwig felt that Cologne was not a neat, smiling city like Bonn. He didn't care for it at all.

When they arrived at the inn, Johann said to Ludwig, "Unpack our box. I am going to see if the Cologne newspaper, the *Kölnische Zeitung,* has printed my advertisement. And I'll put up our placard outside the concert hall."

Johann then disappeared. The afternoon passed slowly for Ludwig. When his father came back, they had soup and bread. And then it was time to get ready for the concert.

Ludwig had a hard time putting on his new clothes. He tore the satin knickers, when he pulled them over his buckled shoes. He buttoned his waistcoat crooked. The tight wig gave him a headache. Johann was no help, he was too busy making himself handsome.

They walked to the concert hall. People were straggling in. A few were richly dressed, but most wore plain, everyday clothes.

"Did you hear that man with pointed mustaches as we came in, Ludwig?" asked Johann when they were inside. "He was making bets on Mozart against you. He says that when Mozart was six he heard him play, and he is willing to bet ten florins that you are not as good." Ludwig got a cold, sick feeling way down in his stomach.

The feeling grew worse when he had to walk out on the stage. He thought of a line he had written in his copybook in school. Under his breath he said to himself:

"Man, help thyself."

Awkwardly, he bowed to right and to left. Though the hall was cold, he felt himself perspiring. His dark face glistened with sweat, while his hands were icy. He stumbled blindly to the piano and sat down with a clatter.

"Go on, play!" whispered Johann from the wings. Obediently Ludwig played. But a big drop of perspiration splashed from his chin to the keys, then another. Someone in the

front row giggled. He tried to wipe his forehead on his sleeve, and pushed his wig
crooked. A lock of black hair escaped. Then
the people all laughed.

"Go on playing!" ordered Johann furi-
ously.

Ludwig played on, but the audience was
not listening. When he finished, there were
no cries of "Encore!" A few pairs of hands
clapped politely. But that was all. The little
boy hurried from the stage.

Johann had boasted in Bonn that the lords
and ladies of Cologne would give Ludwig
rich presents and great sums of money. But
he knew now that there would be no presents
and very little money. He was so disappointed, he never stopped to think how Ludwig must be feeling.

Ludwig was disappointed too, and angry,
but for a different reason. People had laughed
at him! It was bad enough when the boys at
school did so, as they often did. But to be
laughed at by grownups was too much. Besides, he had played well. He knew he had.
Yet they had not taken the trouble to listen.

Johann spoke no word of comfort. When
the hall was empty, he took Ludwig roughly
by the arm. "We can go now," he said. He

took such long, angry steps on the silent walk back to the inn that Ludwig could hardly keep up with him. In their room he gave the boy a push that sent him reeling.

"Where's your tongue, eh?" he stormed. "You haven't said a word to excuse yourself. What did you do to make them laugh, Dummkopf?"

"I don't know," stammered Ludwig. "I don't know, Papa. I played well, didn't I?"

"They laughed at you," said Johann cruelly. "I've had all my trouble for nothing." He gave Ludwig a box on the ear. "Take that," he said. "You're no Mozart, that's certain. We can't go on a tour. You didn't make enough money."

Ludwig rubbed his smarting cheek. He wondered miserably why Papa couldn't say a comforting word. "Man, help thyself," he whispered again under his breath.

"What did you say?" roared Papa.

"Nothing. Nothing," said the boy.

"No supper for you, sir," said Johann, ripping Ludwig's coat from his back and throwing it over a chair. "You can go to bed. I'm going out. Tomorrow morning early, we'll go back to Bonn."

Alone and supperless, Ludwig crept into

bed. He was hungry and miserable. He felt hurt because people had laughed. But he knew that his music had been good, and that was what he really cared about. And he was glad Johann had not whipped him. He was glad that he was going home, to his mother, to Bonn, away from the cruel, laughing faces in Cologne. As he went to sleep, he told himself, "I'm not Mozart. I'm Beethoven. Perhaps some day, I'll be as good as Mozart."

CHAPTER SIX

No More School!

AFTER the concert in Cologne, Johann kept Ludwig at his music harder than ever.

"Maybe I don't know enough to teach him," he told Maria. "Maybe it wasn't entirely his fault. I'm going to let others make him into a wonder-child if they can."

He engaged other music teachers for Ludwig. One of them was Herr Tobias Pfeiffer, a rollicking young actor who came to board with the Beethovens in 1779. He would come home after playing his part on the stage of the Elector's theater, and would give Ludwig a piano lesson in the middle of the night. But that didn't bother Ludwig, who was used to midnight lessons.

Herr Pfeiffer played the flute, and he taught Ludwig to accompany him on the

piano. Sometimes he brought a violinist
home with him. Then they would play trios.
Sometimes Ludwig's father would sing with
them, and would whack Ludwig for mistakes,
as he always had. But their music sounded so
sweet in the silent night that the neighbors
crept out of bed and stood in the street outside of the Beethoven house to listen.

And then Herr Franz Ries, who lived a
few doors away, gave Ludwig violin lessons.
And an old friend of his grandfather's started
him on the organ.

Ludwig loved the organ. It made such big

sounds. It made him feel warm and sort of quivery. Sometimes he went to church by himself, just to listen to the organ. When it pealed out, he could feel himself flying through the gray stone walls, through the stained glass windows—up, up, up.

One morning, when the service was over, and all the people had gone, Ludwig stayed in his seat. The organist, Father Willibald, looked down from the organ loft. He saw a small figure that looked even smaller in the empty church.

"Good morning, my friend," he called. "Are you waiting to see me?"

Ludwig jumped up. A daring idea struck him.

"Father," he stammered. "Good morning, Father. Could I—may I see the organ, Father?"

"Certainly, my son," replied the monk. "Climb the stairs to the organ loft. I will wait for you."

Ludwig ran up the stairs two at a time. "I play a little," he said breathlessly.

"How old are you?" asked the monk.

"Almost ten," replied Ludwig.

"Well, let me hear what you can do," Father Willibald smiled.

He was amazed when Ludwig put his feet on the right pedals and his hands on the right keys. The boy played a simple piece, but he played it well. Father Willibald saw at once that the dark, eager little boy was a fellow musician.

"Would you like me to teach you the church service?" asked Father Willibald. "Perhaps then, later, if I give you lessons, you will help me at the organ."

"Oh, Father!" was all that Ludwig could say.

In a few short months, he had learned so much that Father Willibald let him play the organ for an occasional service. A Minorite friar also allowed him to play for early mass in the Church of the Minorites. How Ludwig loved that early morning hour in the church!

Every day, after mass, he would rush home from the church, gulp his breakfast, grab his schoolbooks, and run all the way to school. Often he came late, and his teacher, Herr Huppert, gave him a big black mark. Often he was too sleepy to pay attention. Or he daydreamed. Then there were more black marks. No wonder he hated school.

One day, he was looking out of the window at the falling snow, wishing it were time to go home. Suddenly, he heard his name called. Herr Huppert stood on his platform, holding up a copybook for all the class to see. The page was blotted, smeared, and dirty, with badly written words, many of them crossed out.

"I'll dismiss early today any boy who is smart enough to read this," said the teacher. "Would Ludwig Beethoven, my prize student, care to try?"

The whole class could see that it was Ludwig's own copybook! How mean of Herr Huppert to call on him!

"Stand up," said Herr Huppert. "Read so that we can all hear."

Ludwig stood up. But he set his jaw stubbornly. He did not intend to utter a word. He would not give Herr Huppert the satisfaction of making him read the copybook aloud.

"Dummkopf!" said the teacher. "You will stay an hour after school."

There was no help for it, Ludwig would have to stay. He would have to be late for his organ lesson.

Ludwig liked his organ teacher, Herr Neefe, better than all his other music teachers put together. Herr Christian Neefe was the Elector's court organist. He was a small, stoop-shouldered man, not much bigger than Ludwig. But he knew so much!

He had lived in Leipzig, and in other cities in and out of Germany. He told Ludwig stories of the great world outside the walls of Bonn. And he gave him a collection of pieces to practice, called *The Well-Tempered Clavier*. They were by Johann Sebastian Bach. Nobody else in Bonn knew these pieces at that time, but today they are famous.

On this day Ludwig ran all the way from school. When, all out of breath, he came into the Elector's chapel, the little organist was playing. Ludwig knew at once that Herr Neefe was not playing from notes. He was improvising, making up music. "Some day I will improvise too," Ludwig promised himself.

"You are late," said Herr Neefe, looking up from the keys. "But never mind."

"I have brought you a piece I wrote for the organ," said Ludwig. "I showed it to Herr Zenser, the organist of the Münster Church."

"So? And what did he say?" asked Herr Neefe.

"He said, 'You cannot play this. Your hands are too small,'" replied Ludwig.

"So they are," said Herr Neefe, after he had tried a few measures.

"But I will play it when I am bigger," said Ludwig firmly.

"Well, I have something that you can do now," said Herr Neefe, smiling kindly. "The Elector is going away for a few months. I am going with him. While I am gone, I want you to take my place, to play the organ in the Elector's chapel. I appoint you my deputy organist."

Deputy organist! How important that sounded! Ludwig was overjoyed. "But is the Elector willing?" he asked.

Herr Neefe had told the Elector, "If this young genius, Ludwig van Beethoven, goes on as he has begun, he will certainly become a second Mozart." And the Elector had answered, "Then make the education of this boy a matter of special importance." So of course the Elector was willing. He would enjoy the services of "this young genius," and he would not have to pay extra for them.

So, at eleven and a half, Ludwig took Herr Neefe's place at the Elector's organ. When he was there, he could forget the teasing boys in school and the sarcastic teacher, Herr Huppert. The dim light in the chapel, the kindly priest, the familiar smell of the incense, and most of all, the mighty sound of the organ pealing forth at his touch, brought peace. So long as he could make music, little else mattered.

When Herr Neefe returned to Bonn, he kept Ludwig as his assistant organist, without pay. And soon he found more work for his assistant.

"I want you to conduct the rehearsals in the theater," Herr Neefe told him.

This meant that Ludwig would have to play the harpsichord, beat out the measures for the orchestra, and signal to the singers when it was time for them to begin. He would have to be in the theater every morning, after playing for early mass in the chapel.

Ludwig knew that he would have to study

the scores of the operas before he could conduct them. He could not expect grown men to obey a mere boy unless he knew more than they did. He had no time now for anything but music. And so, before his twelfth birthday, he left school.

Now he hardly ever blew out his candle before dawn. Johann did not have to drag him out of bed to work, for he did not go to bed. When he came down in the morning, yawning and heavy-eyed, Maria felt sorry for him, and worried.

"Aren't you working too hard, my son?" she asked anxiously.

"Nonsense," Johann answered for him. "The boy is young and strong. But he ought to be making money. He's doing all this work for nothing."

"We could use money," Maria sighed.

"Ludwig, I have an idea," said Johann. "You have composed three piano sonatas, haven't you? Why not dedicate them to Elector Max Friedrich? Give them to him as a present. That will remind him that you are working for him. You can write a letter to go with the sonatas."

"You write it," said Ludwig sleepily.

"All right. I will," said Johann, always interested in a way to make money without working for it.

Johann wrote a letter that was full of flattering words. He used his old trick, and wrote that Ludwig was only eleven, though by this time, he was thirteen. Ludwig signed the letter without even reading it.

By the time the Elector's answer came, Ludwig had almost forgotten the whole business. His sonatas were graciously accepted. But there was not a word about money.

The following year, Ludwig himself petitioned the Elector Max Friedrich:

"Permit me to be your official assistant court organist."

His request was granted. When Max Friedrich died six weeks later, and a new Elector ruled Bonn, Ludwig's name already had been placed on the salary list.

"I am to have 150 florins a year (75 dollars)," he told his mother proudly. "It's all for you."

"My boy!" Maria's voice trembled. She was glad and sorry, both at the same time, that her Ludwig was doing a man's work. Where would it lead him?

CHAPTER SEVEN

An Unforgettable Meeting

THE BEETHOVEN family sat at supper in the fading twilight. While Maria ladled soup from her kettle into Ludwig's plate, Johann, Karl, and young Johann watched her hungrily.

Ludwig, now a husky boy of seventeen, reached across the table for the loaf of black bread. He tore off a big piece with such force that he knocked the ladle out of Maria's hand. Hot soup splashed on the table. Without waiting for his mother to mop it up, he gulped down a dripping spoonful from his plate.

"I have to hurry," he said, as well as he could with his mouth full. "I have to give a lesson."

"Eat plenty of soup," said Maria. "It's all we have." She sighed as she refilled his plate.

Without Ludwig's earnings, they would not have even soup. Ludwig ate quickly.

"Ludwig!" His mother exclaimed. "You've spilled soup down the front of your only coat. Here, let me—" She laid down her soup ladle, and scrubbed at the spot with a damp dish towel.

"Bother the coat," Ludwig said. "I've finished."

He rose from the table, took his mother's dish towel from her, and mopped at his coat clumsily, wondering as he did so how he should tell her what was in his mind.

He wanted to go away from Bonn. For many months he had dreamed of going to the beautiful Austrian city of Vienna to study with Mozart.

"Better say nothing this evening," he thought. For his mother was having one of her bad coughing spells. Although it was spring, she could not lose that cough. Ludwig patted her on the back, and laid her shawl on her shoulders.

"Help Mamma," he told Karl and Johann before he hurried off to work.

For some time, he had been putting away whatever extra money he could earn, a few

pennies at a time, in a box labeled, "Mozart."
Now, as he walked down the familiar Rheingasse in the soft spring evening, he did sums
in his head. Ludwig was no good at sums.
But he did not have to be good to know that
there were not enough pennies in the box for
coach fare to Vienna.

"I shall have to wait," he thought impatiently.

He did not have to wait long. The following week, after rehearsal at the theater, Herr
Neefe beckoned him backstage.

"Here we can be alone," he said. "I have
brought something for you, Ludwig." He
handed Ludwig a thick letter. "From His
Highness the Elector of Bonn," he said, his
eyes twinkling.

"For me? From the Elector? What have I
done that was wrong?" Ludwig took the letter
by one corner.

"Open it," said Herr Neefe, sitting down
comfortably on a piece of scenery. "It won't
bite."

Ludwig sat down beside him. He opened
the letter. He drew out a clinking purse and a
sealed envelope.

"The envelope—the envelope is addressed

[53]

to Herr Wolfgang Amadeus Mozart." Ludwig's voice was small and breathless.

"It is your letter of introduction, my boy," said Herr Neefe, patting him affectionately on the shoulder. "I have told the Elector of your ambition to study with Mozart. He sends you coach fare and his best wishes."

"Thank you, Herr Neefe." It was hard for Ludwig to say, "Thank you," for he was too proud to ask for favors. But Herr Neefe could see that he was very happy.

"You are to leave for Vienna as soon as possible," said Herr Neefe.

"And my family?" asked Ludwig.

"They will be taken care of."

And so it happened that in May, 1787, the

seventeen-year-old country boy climbed eagerly into the coach that was to carry him to Austria, to the enchanted city of Vienna, and to Mozart.

For eight long days he sat in the jogging coach. He had never been more than a few miles from Bonn, and then Papa had been with him. He was too shy to talk to anyone in the coach. But his heart was singing for joy.

When the beautiful city, with its glistening cathedral spire and its tall palaces came into view, he felt very small and very frightened. He kept touching the precious letter in his pocket. It gave him courage.

The coach rolled to a stop. He climbed

out, stretched his legs, and asked the way to Mozart's house. With thumping heart, he knocked. A servant came to the door.

"Please give this letter to Herr Mozart," said Ludwig timidly.

"Wait here." The man closed the door. Ludwig waited. After some minutes, the door opened again.

"Herr Mozart regrets he cannot see you today," said the servant. "He has had bad news. His father in Salzburg is very ill. He says will you please come back two weeks from today, at six o'clock."

Two weeks to wait! Ludwig's heart sank. Evidently, Mozart was not as anxious to see him as he was to see Mozart.

"Man, help thyself," he reminded himself as he turned away. He found the cheapest room he could. He knew nobody in Vienna. For two weeks, he walked alone through the streets of the beautiful city, hardly seeing the palaces which lined them. He brushed against people from every country in the world, and was too shy to talk to them. He lived on bread and water.

At last he raised the knocker of the Mozart door once more. The same servant answered.

"Please tell Herr Mozart I am here," said Ludwig, his voice hoarse from nervousness.

"Who shall I say?" asked the man, looking down his nose at Ludwig's ill-fitting, dark woolen suit and heavy shoes.

"Ludwig van Beethoven. Don't you remember me? Herr Mozart is expecting me."

"The master is dressing to go out," said the man doubtfully. "But you can wait here." He did not call Ludwig "sir" as he showed him into a small room, with a piano in one corner. As if drawn by a magnet, Ludwig went straight to the piano. He struck a few chords. Now he felt more at home.

He heard the sound of voices, and of a door opening and closing. Then Mozart, alone, came with quick, nervous footsteps into the room.

"What a little man! Even smaller than I am!" was Ludwig's first thought. And indeed, Mozart's body looked too small and frail to carry the large, white-wigged head on top of it. But how gorgeously he was dressed, in a scarlet brocaded coat! Lace ruffles fell softly from the wrists; a gold watch chain reached from pocket to pocket; diamond buttons glittered. Ludwig blinked, and twisted his

[57]

broad hands. He felt very shy and shabby.

"Good evening, Beethoven." Mozart eyed the stocky, broad body, the swarthy face topped with a mop of black hair, and the untamed dark eyes. He liked the eyes.

"I'm sorry I had to keep you waiting," he apologized. "I was dressing. My wife and some friends are waiting for me to go to the opera. To tell the truth, I forgot I had told you to come this evening."

"Another time?" asked Ludwig faintly.

"No, I have a few minutes now. Please play something," said Mozart, restlessly turning over the music on the piano. With his hands on the keys, Ludwig was himself. He played his best. But he could hear Mozart jingling his watch chain, and tapping his foot.

"Very good," said Mozart, but his voice was cool. He considered Ludwig no better than the other young pianists who flocked to him with carefully prepared pieces.

"Please, Herr Mozart, give me a melody," begged Ludwig. "I would like to improvise for you. I will show you what I can do, making up the music as I go along."

Mozart, too, liked to improvise. He was glad to grant Ludwig's request. Seating himself at the piano, he played a portion of one of his own compositions. He chose a hard one. He knew that only a fine musician would be able to pick out the melody cleverly concealed in it. This was a real test.

Ludwig listened attentively. He sat down at the piano. He played Mozart's melody through. He twisted and turned it, played it in different keys, different rhythms, with different harmonies. He forgot the people in the

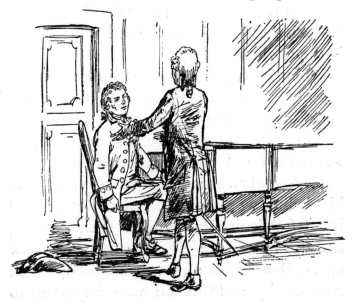

next room. He forgot the opera Mozart was going to. He played on and on.

Mozart forgot too. He recognized something in Ludwig's music, something that was different, stronger, bigger even than his own.

[59]

He embraced Ludwig, and kissed him on both cheeks.

"I will help you. You shall be my pupil," he promised.

So joyful that he hardly knew what he was doing, Ludwig mumbled a few words of thanks, and made for the door. He forgot his hat.

Mozart hurried excitedly to his friends in the next room. "Did you hear that?" he asked. "Watch that young man; he will make a noise in the world some day."

When Ludwig reached his little room, he executed a clumsy bear-dance of joy. He hoped that his first lesson would be soon. But although he had won Mozart's approval, he was not to be Mozart's pupil after all.

He waited two months, anxiously counting his dwindling store of pennies. But Mozart had left Vienna shortly after their meeting and did not return for some time. His new opera, *Don Giovanni,* was being produced in another city, and this was more important to him than teaching the young pianist from Bonn.

At the end of the two months, Ludwig received a sad letter from Bonn.

"Your mother is very ill," Johann wrote.

"If you wish to see her alive, come home at once."

With a heavy heart, Ludwig climbed into the coach. How different the return trip was from his journey to Vienna, so full of hope!

When he reached home, he found his mother in bed, too weak to move. He raised her on her pillow. She laid her head on his broad shoulder.

"You—must be—the head of the family," she whispered. "Promise me—promise—take care—Karl—Johann—Margaretha."

Through his tears, Ludwig promised.

"You have been such a kind, loving mother to me, and my best friend," he sobbed, as he laid her gently back on her pillow.

After her death, he became very ill too. But he kept his promise to her as soon as he could. At seventeen, he had to be mother as well as father to twelve-year-old Karl, ten-year-old Johann, and the year-old baby sister Margaretha whimpering in her cradle.

Big Johann was no help at all. He did no work. He never came home except to sleep. He expected Ludwig to take care of everything. And Ludwig did.

He moved the family out of the neglected rooms in the Rheingasse to a pleasanter apartment in the Wenzelgasse. He engaged a woman to look after Karl and Johann. Baby Margaretha could not live without her mother's love and care. She died shortly after Maria. Ludwig decided that red-haired little Karl was to be a musician, and dark, handsome Johann a chemist. As soon as he could, he apprenticed them both to study their trade.

Now again he went daily to the organ in the Elector's chapel. When Herr Neefe retired, the Elector appointed Ludwig court pianist. He put on the Elector's green-and-gold livery, and played the viola in the Elector's orchestra. And he started to compose in real earnest.

He was becoming a somebody in Bonn. He felt strong and powerful, able to take care of his family and still live his own life as he wished. Many pupils came to him. Among them, he made friends, the first real, live friends he had ever had. The next five years in Bonn were busy and happy.

CHAPTER EIGHT

Farewell to Bonn

MY NEW pupil, Eleonore von Breuning, is doing fine. And she's pretty, too."

Ludwig threw down his green uniform coat on a kitchen chair, and walked over to the table where his brother Johann sat pouring a yellow liquid from one bottle into another. Johann was now twelve, Ludwig nineteen.

"What are you doing, Johann?" asked Ludwig in his best older-brother tone. "Will that stuff explode?"

"I'm doing a chemistry experiment," replied Johann. "No, it won't explode."

Ludwig laid on the table the heavy book he had been carrying under his arm.

"Want to read my book?" he asked. "Eleonore's mother, Frau von Breuning, loaned it to me. It's a story by a Greek named Homer."

"Not I," scoffed Johann. "You and your dull books. You and your music. You and your Von Breunings. That's all you talk about."

"I have good times with the Von Breunings." Ludwig turned the pages of the book while he talked. "They have given me a second home. I believe I like Eleonore's mother even better than I like Eleonore. She keeps me from missing Mamma so much." His face grew sad for a moment.

"Her house is so friendly, and the door is always open to me. There are beautiful paintings on the walls, and flowers in every room, and so many books I'll never be able to read them all! In the evenings, she often reads poetry aloud to the whole family."

"What a bore!" said young Johann.

"Frau von Breuning is like a mother to me in every way," continued Ludwig, paying no attention to his brother's remark. "She even sews on my buttons when they come off, great lady though she is. She insists that I must dress properly and behave correctly, and she shows me how. I do love her!"

"Who cares?" asked Johann rudely.

"Next Sunday, the whole Von Breuning

family—Eleonore and her three brothers, Christoph, Stephan, and little Lorenz—Lenz they call him—and of course, their mother, are going up the river for a picnic. Franz Wegeler and Count von Waldstein are going too," continued Ludwig.

He laid aside the book and sat down at the table.

"I'm invited," he said happily. "Don't you wish you could go too?"

"Well—yes," Johann confessed. "But can you get away?" he asked, a trifle enviously.

"I'll get someone to play the organ in my place that day," replied Ludwig. "Frau von Breuning warned me to be on time. She said, 'See that you are not in your *raptus* on Sunday morning.'"

Ludwig threw his broad body back in the kitchen chair and slapped his thigh, laughing loudly.

"What does *that* mean?" asked Johann.

"Well, when I am writing a new piece of music, or just do not feel like teaching, I sometimes don't show up at Eleonore's lesson time," Ludwig confessed. "Then Frau von Breuning tells her, 'Never mind, Lorchen, Ludwig is in his *raptus* again.' It's a word she made up."

"Ach, a crazy word," said Johann, holding a test tube to the light.

"I like it," replied Ludwig cheerfully.

He got up and put on his coat.

"Tell Karl I won't be home till late," he said. "I have a class at the university, a lecture Frau von Breuning thinks I ought to hear."

Ludwig, who had never even finished grammar school, was now going to college. He was thrilled when one of his professors there told his class about the American Revolutionary War which had begun when he was only six. And of the French Revolution which started soon after and was still going on.

"All men are created free and equal. All are entitled to Liberty, Equality, and Brotherhood. These are the ideas men fight for," said the professor.

Ludwig wanted to talk over these new ideas. His friends were of the nobility, and he was not. But when he was with them, he felt free and equal. He waited eagerly for the day of the picnic. But on that sparkling Sunday morning in May, who could be serious?

After a merry boat ride up the river, the gay party landed at a farm belonging to Frau von Breuning's brother. Little Lenz spied a cherry orchard heavy with ripe fruit.

"Let's picnic under the cherry trees!" he cried.   . .

Frau von Breuning and Eleonore spread a white cloth under a cherry tree. While the boys gathered baskets of fruit, they brought out good things from the hampers. Soon all were seated on the ground, eating and drinking. Such wonderful roast chicken and white bread, such sweet cakes, such good Bonn Rhine wine! The food was very different from the black bread and soup on the Beethoven table. Ludwig ate and drank till he could hold no more.

After lunch, the others went off to explore the woods. Ludwig sat down by himself, his back against a tree. He drew a notebook from his pocket. He always carried a notebook and pencil with him, so that he could write down the music that kept coming into his mind. That was his habit, all his life long.

But today he was to write no music. For Eleonore came dancing by his tree. She dangled a big, juicy cherry teasingly before him.

"Come and get it," she invited.

As he reached for it, she stepped aside. He stood up and tried again. Because of her wide skirts, he could not come close. She ran away, keeping a step or two ahead of him as he chased her clumsily. He could not catch her.

Her brother Stephan saw that Ludwig was embarrassed. "Wait, I'll catch her for you," he laughed. He headed his sister off and held her tight while Ludwig grabbed the cherry.

"Lorchen's a tease," Stephan said, as he let her go with a brotherly smack.

"Thank you, Stephan," panted Ludwig.

That evening, when they were all grouped around the Von Breuning piano, he started a new game to please her.

"Guess who this is," he said. On the spot he played a piece that described someone in the room. He was imitating a person in music. Sometimes they could guess whom he meant, sometimes they could not. But everyone liked the new game, especially when Ludwig went wandering off into exquisite melodies that enchanted them.

As time went on, the fame of Ludwig's

improvisations—as they were called—spread beyond Bonn. Travelers from other cities, who came to Bonn, would ask to hear young "Bethoven," or "Biethoffen," or "Bathoven." They all spelled the name differently. Ludwig didn't always spell it the same way himself.

One day, a very special visitor came to Bonn. It was "Papa" Haydn. He had been there two years before, at Christmas time, on his way to London. One of his Masses had been performed in the Elector's chapel at that time, and Ludwig had never forgotten it. Now, in July, Haydn again stopped in Bonn on his way home from London. He had once asked, "Who is this Ludwig, anyway?" This

time, his question would be answered, and his visit would change Ludwig's whole life.

Ludwig was twenty-two. As he sat at the organ in the Elector's chapel that July morning, he felt discontented.

"What am I doing in Bonn?" he asked himself restlessly. "Bonn is too small for me. It's like a suit that I've grown out of. If only I could have stayed in Vienna with Mozart! Alas, I can never study with him now. Poor Mozart! To die when he was only thirty-five!"

Thinking of Mozart made Ludwig think of "Papa" Haydn, Mozart's good friend and favorite composer. "I will play something of Haydn's today," he mused. "His music is full of melodies, like Mozart's."

When it was time for the service, Ludwig played an organ prelude by Haydn. The tones pealed out. They filled the dim church with glorious sound. Now Ludwig no longer felt unhappy.

After the service, he went to the little room behind the altar to wait for some of his friends. But when the door opened, it was the Elector who entered. With his coming, life and color streamed into the gray little room. Courtiers in purple and golden and crimson satins and velvets crowded behind their ruler.

Among them was a smiling little man dressed all in black. Snowy lace ruffles at his neck and wrists, and a snowy white wig with three rolls on each side of his face made his black suit look blacker. It was Haydn himself.

"Beethoven, I wish to present you to our Haydn, whom you respect so deeply," said the Elector graciously.

Ludwig remembered seeing Haydn two years before, but he was sure that Haydn did not remember seeing him.

"I—I hope you liked—" he stammered.

"You play the organ well, young man." Haydn's black eyes twinkled and his cheeks creased when he smiled.

With sudden courage, Ludwig said, "I compose music too. May I show you something?"

"After dinner, after dinner," said the Elector testily. The Elector had planned a dinner party for Haydn. The Elector loved to eat.

"After dinner then, Your Highness," said Haydn, bowing.

"Come along to dinner, Beethoven," said the Elector graciously.

After dinner, Ludwig placed on the table before Haydn the score of a cantata he had composed. It was a work for solo voices, chorus, and orchestra. Haydn examined it carefully.

"Hm," he said. "You have talent, more than enough. A little wild and uncontrolled. If you knew a little more about the rules of composition, it would do no harm. See that you make sure of coming to Vienna."

Ludwig's eyes opened wide. Had Haydn read his mind? Of course he wished to go to Vienna, but how could he? Haydn left Bonn the very next day, but Ludwig told the Von Breunings and Count Waldstein what he had said.

Count Waldstein was a great friend of Ludwig's. He had made him a present of a new piano, which he sorely needed, for Grandfather's was quite worn out. He had sent him pupils, as many as Ludwig had time for. He had invited visitors from other cities to hear Ludwig improvise, and they had gone back home and talked about the wonderful young musician of Bonn.

Years later, Ludwig said "Thank you" to Count Waldstein in a beautiful piano sonata, now known as the *Waldstein Sonata*. He could say "Thank you" in music much better than in words. "I would rather write ten thousand notes of music than one letter of the alphabet," he told his friend.

Now Count Waldstein persuaded the Elector to grant Ludwig a long leave of absence with pay, so that he could go to Vienna to study with Haydn. The count persuaded the Elector to provide for Ludwig's family while he was away. These arrangements took time.

One evening, the count appeared at the Von Breuning home, smiling broadly. Ludwig was at the piano. There were many guests. The count made his way to the piano and waited until Ludwig had finished playing.

"Everything is prepared for your departure, Ludwig," he said, laying his hand affectionately on Ludwig's shoulder. "You are to go to

Vienna, where you will receive the spirit of Mozart from the hand of Haydn."

From one pocket, he drew a packet of letters. "These letters will introduce you to the patrons and music lovers of Vienna," he said. From the other pocket, he brought forth a souvenir album. "For you, from your friends in Bonn," he added.

Count Waldstein had let the others in on the secret beforehand. They crowded around the piano. They embraced Ludwig. They gave him parting gifts. Eleonore pressed into his hand a scarf she had knitted for him.

He was sorry to leave his good friends. But he was going to Vienna! A few days later, with a big box of music, Grandfather's portrait, and a small box of clothes, he climbed gaily into the coach. Papa Johann and his brothers Karl and Johann did not see him off. But his friends were there. They had written loving messages in his souvenir album.

"Do not forget us!" they cried.

"I will never forget you," he swore.

His heart swelled as he said good-by to them; to the little town of Bonn; to his teachers; and to the river Rhine that he loved so well. He did not know that it was to be good-by forever.

[*74*]

CHAPTER NINE

Vienna, the Enchanted City

HOW busy everybody in Vienna is!"

Ludwig looked out of the window of his tiny room above a printer's shop. The bustling crowds below looked like many-colored insects, pushing and crowding, humming and buzzing.

"Soon I'll be just as busy as they are." Ludwig talked to Grandfather's portrait as he hung it above his bed. It kept him company, and made him feel less alone.

"I'll hire a piano at once," he announced to Grandfather. "If my money holds out, I'll buy a new coat, and some silk stockings, and take dancing lessons, as Frau von Breuning said I should. I'll need a wig, too."

He wore his wig, and his new coat, when

he left the letters of introduction Count Waldstein had given him, at the palaces of the important people of Vienna. He wore them when he went sightseeing—to the cathedral with its gilded spire, to the gleaming white Imperial Library, to the Theater an der Wien.

On his first visit to Vienna, to see Mozart, he had walked through the streets with unseeing eyes, too worried and too ignorant to perceive the beauty surrounding him. At that time, he had not yet met the Von Breunings, nor learned from them how to find pleasure in other things than music. Now, he enjoyed everything.

He put a monocle in his eye, like the Viennese dandies, when he went for a Sunday walk in the Prater. The Prater was a great park where, in the afternoon, all Vienna drove or walked. Ludwig stood stock still in amazement when the coach of the Austrian Emperor, drawn by six horses, drove by. It was followed by the rich coaches of the nobility, and the hired carriages of the lesser subjects.

Between gaily attired ladies and gentlemen riding on prancing horses, and smiling citizens on foot, the carriages mingled in a broad, winding parade. The Emperor bowed to his subjects. They bowed to one another.

He saw the cathedral with its gilded spire

Nobody bowed to Ludwig, and he felt very lonely.

He walked and walked. He walked in the city streets, lined with princely palaces. He walked on the Bastion, where there was a platform for outdoor concerts, where flags fluttered and decorated lemonade stands beckoned. And he fell in love with Vienna.

"Here will I stay," he vowed, "and not return to Bonn, even if the Elector cuts off my allowance."

He had always felt more at home with music than with people, and in Vienna he found plenty of music. On street corners, in gardens and courtyards, friend serenaded friend with songs and string quartets. In the State Opera House, he listened to Italian operas he had never heard of before. When he went to the cathedral he listened for the first time to the cantatas of Bach, the oratorios of Handel, and the masses of Mozart.

He had been in Vienna barely a month when he had news from Bonn. "Your father died on December 18," said the message.

Ludwig had no reason to grieve for his shiftless father. Johann had beaten him, had made his mother's life miserable, and had spent on drink the money that should have

gone to feed and clothe his family. Ludwig
had even had to rescue his father from the
police of Bonn when they tried to arrest him
for drunkenness. So the news of his death did
not sadden his son.

"I will bring Karl and Johann to Vienna
when they have finished their apprentice-
ship," he wrote to his relatives in Bonn. And
that being settled, he proceeded to enjoy life
in Vienna.

It was not long before all the nobles who
had received the letters of introduction were
bowing to Ludwig when he took his walks on
the Prater. They invited him to their palaces,
though they thought he was queer. His German was different from theirs. His most elegant clothes were not half as elegant as theirs.
He often wore no wig. He laughed too loudly,
and felt insulted for no reason. But how he
could play the piano!

"It is good to be with the nobility," Ludwig wrote in his notebook, "but one must be
able to impress them."

Impress them he did. Prince Lichnowsky
and his beautiful young wife fell in love with
Ludwig's music. The prince was twenty and
Ludwig was twenty-two. The prince had
studied the violin and piano with Mozart, and

he employed four men to play string quartets. In those days, only the nobles could afford to pay musicians to play for them. There were hardly any public concerts in Vienna.

The Prince and Princess Lichnowsky made Ludwig warmly welcome to their palace in the Älserstrasse, much as Frau von Breuning had done in Bonn. A year passed on golden wings.

"We'd like you to come and live in the palace with us, Beethoven," said the prince one morning after quartet practice.

"Please do," begged the princess.

Ludwig hesitated. He knew that most nobles treated their house musicians like servants. He had made up his mind he would never be a servant, not to Prince Lichnowsky, not to anyone.

"You must understand that you are a prince, but I am Beethoven," was his proud answer.

"I understand," said the prince graciously, as he snapped his violin case shut. "But will you come?"

"I will come," said Ludwig.

He moved his belongings from his bare little room to a silken suite in the Lichnowsky palace. The prince and princess thought nothing was too good for their guest. They made him a present of four beautiful Italian instruments—two violins, a viola, and a cello. They gave him an income of six hundred florins a year ($300). He had his own riding horse, his own servant.

"I'd like to put Herr Beethoven under a glass case and keep him there," said the princess fondly.

Yet Ludwig did not change his habits. He often dressed carelessly, in the comfortable, ugly clothes he had brought from Bonn. Sometimes he did not shave for dinner, even if there were guests. He hated being on time for meals, and often he came late, or went to the coffeehouse to eat. He could be very rude in other ways, too.

One evening, he was playing the piano in the drawing room. While he was playing, a young nobleman in the next room laughed loudly at a joke.

"For such swine I do not play!" exclaimed Ludwig, and left the piano in a huff. He thought the young man was laughing at him, and he could never bear that. Besides, he expected people to listen when he played for them. Though the young man apologized, Beethoven played no more that evening.

The Lichnowskys forgave him this. They forgave him everything.

Twice a week, Ludwig went for lessons to Herr Haydn. This was what he had come to Vienna for. But Herr Haydn often seemed very busy, and Ludwig was disappointed in

his teaching. As he was leaving Herr Haydn's house one day, he met Herr Schenk, a musician whom he knew slightly.

"Good morning," said Herr Schenk politely. "Is it music that I see under your arm?"

"Yes. Some exercises that I prepared for Herr Haydn," replied Ludwig.

"May I see them?" asked Herr Schenk, falling into step beside him.

"Why not?" Ludwig shrugged. "Let's have a cup of coffee. I will show them to you."

They went to a near-by café. Ludwig spread his papers on the table, between their coffee cups.

"Here's a mistake." Herr Schenk pointed to a chord. "And in this passage, you've broken a rule."

"What rule? What mistake?" cried Ludwig. "Haydn has just corrected this exercise. It must be right."

"But it isn't," retorted Herr Schenk. "I am a teacher too."

"Is it for this the Elector sent me to Vienna?" fumed Ludwig. "Haydn does not even correct my mistakes."

"If you wish, I will correct your exercises," said Herr Schenk.

"I am bound to study with Haydn," replied Ludwig. "That is why I am here."

"You can copy the exercises after they are corrected, and take them to Haydn as usual. He need never know," suggested Herr Schenk.

For the next two years, he and other teachers helped Ludwig. Ludwig studied dutifully.

He wanted to learn all the rules. Later, he would break them on purpose, when he felt it was right to do so.

Ludwig had been in Vienna three years when the Lichnowskys gave a big party. Their white and gold salon blazed with candles. Their table was laden with good things to eat. White-wigged flunkies in the prince's livery served the noble guests.

The men who played string quartets at the prince's Friday morning concerts were there, with their instruments. The first violinist, Ignaz Schuppanzigh, a huge, fat man, was Ludwig's special friend. Ludwig nicknamed him Falstaff, after a funny fat man in a play by Shakespeare.

All of the music-loving nobles of Vienna were at the party. Prince Lobkowitz attended, of course, and Baron van Swieten. Count Esterhazy, Haydn's employer, was there with Haydn himself. And there were many others.

There were ladies too, dainty in their hoop skirts trimmed with bows and lacy frills. The curls they wore on each side of their smoothly parted hair bobbed up and down in time with the gold lockets hung around their necks, as they giggled and whispered behind their fans.

After supper, the company went into the grand salon.

"Let us have music!" the prince's booming voice commanded. He singled out Ludwig's black hair among the powdered wigs. "Herr van Beethoven, will you—?"

"Not now, Prince," replied Ludwig unexpectedly. "I'm too sleepy." He yawned, without covering his mouth. He walked over to a couch in the corner of the room, and stretched out on it. His mop of black hair sank into the golden cushion. He closed his eyes.

The princess's mother, the Countess of Thun, a very great lady, came over to the couch. She knelt beside it, took Ludwig's hand, and kissed it. "Do play for us, Herr van Beethoven, won't you please?" she asked sweetly.

Ludwig turned his head away. He pretended to be asleep.

The countess rose. She put her finger on her lips. She shook her head at the company. "It is 'No,' " she whispered.

The members of the string quartet took out their instruments and played a Mozart quartet. When it was finished, the prince made another announcement.

[*85*]

"I have here three trios for piano, violin, and cello," he said, holding up a bulky manuscript. "They are by a young, unknown composer and have not yet been published. Herr Schuppanzigh, will you ask Herr van Beethoven if he is ready now to read the piano part?"

Ludwig was not asleep. He was only pretending. When his friend Falstaff whispered in his ear, "The prince wants us to play your trios," Ludwig was on his feet in a flash. In another flash, he was at the piano, nodding to Falstaff and the cellist to begin.

The room was still. Everyone knew that if

there was a sound during the music, Ludwig would fly out of the room. They were quiet, too, because they really enjoyed the three beautiful trios.

"Bravo, Bravo!" they cried. "Composer! Composer! Who is the composer?"

"Composer! Composer!" cried Haydn, louder than all the rest. He may have guessed the composer's name even before the prince took Ludwig's hand and led him, flushed and excited, to take his bow. Then the clapping was deafening. They all wanted to congratulate Ludwig. But it was to Haydn that he turned first. He had never shown his teacher the trios. He had wanted them to be a surprise.

"I congratulate you, Beethoven," said Haydn. He smiled and twinkled as always, but to Ludwig his smile seemed strained. "I like the first two trios very much," he continued. "But in my opinion the third, the one in C minor, is too hard for an audience to understand."

"Why, that's the one I like most," exclaimed Ludwig. "In *my* opinion, it's the best of the three."

"All the same, if I were you, I wouldn't publish the third," said Haydn mildly.

[*87*]

"Haydn is jealous," thought Ludwig, as he turned away, biting his lip. All the praise he received from the other guests could not take the sting from Haydn's remark.

He was much surprised, when, later in the evening, Haydn came up to him, all smiles.

"By the way, Ludwig," he said, "when you publish those trios you ought to have the title page say, 'Trios by Ludwig van Beethoven, Pupil of Haydn.' "

"Aha! So Haydn thinks well enough of the trios to want his name to appear on them," was Ludwig's first thought. "Pupil of Haydn! I never learned anything from you!" was his second thought. He did not say it, but his eyes flashed. Haydn felt uncomfortable. He turned to Count Esterhazy. "Beethoven seems to think he is the Great Mogul," he remarked, as they walked away together.

"Ha, a good name for him," chuckled the count.

Centuries earlier, the Great Mogul had conquered the whole continent of Europe by the sword. Now, Ludwig van Beethoven, twenty-five years old, was preparing to conquer it with his music.

CHAPTER TEN

"Great Mogul" of Vienna

AT TWENTY-FIVE, Ludwig had already composed music that made those who heard it exclaim, "Wunderbar!" He already played the piano better than any of the other three hundred pianists in Vienna. He gave lessons to the wives and daughters of princes. He had every right to be proud of what he had done.

One day he left the Lichnowsky palace and moved into a room of his own. Here he could be free, as he wished to be. Here he could shave or not, dress or not, eat or not, sleep or not, talk or not, work or not, as he pleased.

One morning, he had just taken up his pen and settled down at his desk when there came a knock at his door.

"Come in," he growled.

"A messenger has brought a letter for you,

sir." It was his landlord, timidly sticking his head in at the door. The landlord was afraid to come in. He knew how much Ludwig hated to be interrupted.

Ludwig frowned and stretched out his hand, without looking up.

"Give it here," he said rudely. The man handed it to him, and went quickly out of the room.

Ludwig did not know how much he frightened people. Because he was such a great genius, he was annoyed by things that ordinary people pay no attention to. At such times, he could be very rude. He roared, and threw things, and quarreled with his best friends. They usually forgave him because of his genius, and because they loved him, and because he begged them to forgive him. But they would not have forgiven anyone else who behaved as Ludwig sometimes did.

He stopped frowning when he read the letter. It was an invitation, but it was not signed by a prince or a duke. It invited him to play his own compositions at a *public* concert.

There were no regular public concerts in Vienna in those days. There was no regular orchestra. It had been Ludwig's good fortune that the nobles, who employed their own orchestras and string quartets, had placed them at his disposal. Because he had played only in their palaces, only the nobles knew his music.

But at this concert, shopkeepers, artisans, and working people would buy tickets for charity. There was to be a specially engaged orchestra. And best of all, the concert would be, not in a prince's palace, but in the Burgtheater, a large hall. Ludwig was delighted.

"Ludwig van Beethoven accepts with pleasure," he wrote in his untidy scrawl.

"I will write a new piano concerto," he said aloud, pushing aside the piece he was working on. He was already writing twelve German

[*91*]

dances for orchestra, a set of minuets for piano, and a trio. But didn't he always work on several things at a time? Yes, he could write a concerto before the date of the concert, March 29, 1795.

But time flew. All of a sudden, the concert was only a week off. Then, two days before the great day, Ludwig woke up feeling very ill. He often had stomach attacks because he had eaten the wrong things and had worked too hard while he was a boy in Bonn. But this time, it was especially bad. Oh, what a stomach-ache he had! And his piano concerto was still not finished. He sent his servant running for a doctor.

"As soon as you have found a doctor," he moaned, "go out again and find me four music copyists."

Ludwig lay in bed, doubled up with pain. The doctor worked over him with pills and poultices. The four copyists sat around a table near the bed, quill pens in hand, sand-shaker ready, inkpot in the middle.

Between groans, Ludwig composed the third and last movement of his *B Flat Piano Concerto*. It is the merriest movement of all. To hear it, nobody would think that the composer had an ache or a pain.

As fast as he finished a page, he tossed it to the copyists. They wrote out the parts for the different instruments of the orchestra. They sanded the wet ink, and laid the sheets in an orderly pile. The pile grew higher. The sun sank lower. And the concerto was finished.

On the day before the concert, Ludwig, weak and wobbly, rehearsed in his room with the orchestra. But what was this? The A of his piano was not the same as the A of the orchestra's oboe. The strings were tuned according to the oboe, so the orchestra sounded a half tone higher than the piano.

Ludwig's ear told him that he would have to play his part a half tone higher. He would have to transpose it to the key of B, with five sharps, instead of B-flat, which has two flats. This was a difficult feat, but not too difficult for Ludwig. He transposed while he played. The orchestra men applauded him. And at the performance, the concerto went superbly.

"Bravo, Beethoven, bravo!" cried the audience.

"Bravo, Beethoven, bravo!" cried the newspaper critics.

"The master hand of Ludwig van Beethoven pleased the people of Vienna," was their verdict.

Now Ludwig was not only the Great Mogul of the nobles. He was the Great Mogul of Vienna too.

With his pupils, he acted truly like the Great Mogul. One day, he walked with his friend, Stephan von Breuning, down the Allee-strasse. Stephan had come to Vienna to practice law. Ludwig usually took his daily walk by himself, scribbling in his notebook as he went. He never missed that walk, rain or shine. Today, he was to give a lesson to Tesi von Brunswick, one of his favorite pupils.

"Come, walk with me to the Hotel Golden Dragon," said Ludwig. "I go there to teach the daughters of the Countess von Brunswick."

"Are the girls good pianists?" asked Stephan.

"Hm, yes. Tesi plays the piano part of my trio and sings the violin and cello parts correctly at the same time," said Ludwig approvingly. "She even practices at night sometimes after the others are asleep."

"She must like her teacher," said Stephan teasingly.

"Ha, perhaps." Ludwig liked to be teased about a pretty girl. He had been in love very often, but never for more than a few months at a time. The two friends parted at the hotel.

"Good day," said Ludwig to the landlord standing at the door.

The man gave him a sour look. His guests were complaining that the piano playing in the Von Brunswick apartment disturbed them. Besides, Ludwig often stayed so long teaching that the landlord had to serve dinner at five instead of the usual hour of two. But a landlord did not carry complaints to the wealthy Countess von Brunswick about the Great Mogul Ludwig van Beethoven.

Ludwig mounted the stairs two at a time. As he came close to the door, he heard the sound of someone practicing. He stopped to listen, smiled, then frowned. The notes were correct, but Tesi was not playing the passages of his sonata loud and soft where he had marked them so. He knocked. The piece was stopped midway. He heard an "Oh!" and the swish of silken skirts. Tesi opened the door.

"Herr van Beethoven! I did not expect you so early!" she exclaimed.

"So you are doing your practicing now, eh?" he said.

"I couldn't before. I was at a ball till early this morning," she excused herself.

"Whatever you do, never let your other oc-

[95]

cupations make you neglect the piano, or indeed the whole of music generally," he said gravely. Tesi hung her head.

"Well, sit down. Let me hear the sonata," he said, throwing his hat on a chair and his coat on top of it. Tesi opened the music on the rack.

"You haven't yet learned it by heart?" he asked, displeased. "Well, play from the notes then."

At the end of the first page, he started to walk up and down impatiently. When Tesi played the second page, he stopped her to correct her. At the end of the third, he seized the music, tore it in half, and threw it in her lap. With a snort, he snatched up his hat and coat, and stalked out of the room.

Tesi burst into tears. Her mother, the countess, ran in from the next room.

"Herr Beethoven didn't mean to hurt you," she soothed. "You know how suddenly he gets angry, and how sweet he is afterward."

"But he is so wonderful," sobbed Tesi. "I hate to displease him."

"Stop crying. Your eyes will be all red and swollen," said the practical countess. "You can paste the music together, and it will be as good as new. He will be back tomorrow, you know."

Meanwhile, Ludwig was taking a long walk around the Bastion. As soon as he was out of the house, he forgot Tesi von Brunswick. He took from his pocket the notebook he always had with him. He called it his "banner," waving for all the world to see. As he walked, he wrote music in it. His writing was so jiggly that only he could read it.

It started to rain. He did not notice it. Suddenly, he found that his pencil was not making a mark on the paper. The notebook was sopping wet. It was no use to write any more, so he turned his steps homeward. In the hall of his house, he shook himself like a shaggy dog, and drained the water from his hat onto the floor.

"Please to dry yourself outside," called a man's voice. His landlord appeared in the hall. "Oh, it's you, Herr Beethoven. I might have known it," he said crossly. "Look at the mess you've made again. My wife will have to mop up the hall."

"If you don't like it, I can move," said Ludwig loftily.

"No, sir, excuse me, sir," said the man. "I only came out to tell you that there is a visitor for you. He has a great big instrument with him. It was raining so hard, I told him to wait for you in your room."

"Who is he? What is his name?" asked Ludwig, as he started up the stairs.

"Dragon—Dragonetti—or something like that," said the man.

"Dragonetti!" Ludwig quickened his steps. Dragonetti was a renowned concert artist. He played the double bass, an unusual instrument. He was famous all over Europe. A visit from him was an event—if it *was* Dragonetti.

His visitor rose as Ludwig entered the room. Even standing, he looked small beside his huge instrument, which he had propped against the wall. It was much taller than he.

"Sir, I am honored. Please be seated." Ludwig bowed lower to a fellow artist than to any king. He threw off his wet coat, brushed papers off the table, and called the landlord to bring coffee. In a few minutes, the two men were dunking coffee cake into their cups and talking like old friends.

"Would you like to play something?" asked Ludwig presently.

"That is why I brought my instrument," said Dragonetti, smiling. "Something of yours, please, Herr van Beethoven."

The double bass is hardly ever played as a solo instrument, for the tone is thick and growly, and the instrument hard to handle.

"I'll give him something difficult," said Ludwig to himself. "A real test."

He chuckled as he placed before Dragonetti the music of his *Cello Sonata in G Minor*. It contains tricky, fast passages which are difficult for the cello, and much more difficult for the overgrown cello known as a double bass. Dragonetti had to stand while he played, in order that his left hand could reach the strings on the fingerboard.

To Ludwig's amazement, the passages flowed smoothly from Dragonetti's nimble fingers. Halfway through, there was a very fast section. Dragonetti whizzed up and down his instrument like a breeze. Ludwig jumped up from the piano bench. He rushed over to Dragonetti. He took the player and his unwieldy instrument into a big bearlike embrace.

"How do you do it?" he exclaimed, "Show me!"

Dragonetti smilingly rescued his instrument from Ludwig's hug. He showed him how he handled the short, thick bow and the long, thick strings to bring out a melody. This was one music lesson that Ludwig never forgot. He remembered it especially when, years later, he wrote a melody for double basses in his last and greatest symphony, the *Ninth*.

Dragonetti was one of many distinguished visitors who knocked at Ludwig's door during the ten happy years when he was the Great Mogul of Vienna. At the end of the ten years, a terrible misfortune awaited him.

CHAPTER ELEVEN

Courage!

IT WAS a soft, sunshiny day in May, 1802. Ludwig was in the country, at a farmhouse in Heiligenstadt. The village, which he dearly loved, was just outside Vienna. That morning early, his favorite pupil, Fritz Ries, had come from Vienna for a lesson with the Master. The seventeen-year-old Fritz was the son of Ludwig's old violin teacher in Bonn. Fritz was an early riser, and arrived shortly after breakfast, but Ludwig, also an early riser, was ready for him.

"Look, Fritz," said Ludwig, standing at the door and pointing. "How lovely the valley is today. It is so clear that you can see the Carpathian Mountains in the distance. Let's take a walk before we work."

Gladly Fritz put down his music. They

walked all morning, Ludwig trotting fast, a
few steps ahead of his companion. He
hummed snatches of song, waved his arms in
the air, and stopped now and again to make
notes in his book. He seemed to forget that
Fritz was with him.

At noon, they found themselves at the en-
trance to a cozy inn. A brook ran chattering
through the garden. Ducks swam in a pond.

"Here will we eat," said Ludwig. He
stooped to let the water in the brook run
through his fingers. He dearly loved the sight
and sound of cool running water.

They sat down at a table under an apple
tree in rosy bloom. A fat waiter brought sau-
sages and sauerkraut, cheese, and steins of cold
beer. Ludwig sighed aloud with contentment.

He spoke about his work. "I have more orders than I can fill, and six or seven publishers for each of my works," he told Fritz happily. He went on to tell about a concert tour he had made.

"When I was twenty-six, I played in Prague, and Nürnberg, and Berlin, all big cities," he recalled. "In Berlin, the King of Germany made me a present of a box filled with gold pieces. It was no ordinary box, let me tell you, but one of the kind given only to important ambassadors." Fritz listened eagerly. How wonderful his master was!

"We will have to go," said Ludwig at last, throwing back his head to drain the last drop of beer. "It's a long way home. Fritz, please add up the bill. I have no head for figures. If I have to multiply 24 by 13, I write down 24's in a column, 13 of them, and then add them."

"It's easy when you know how," said Fritz modestly. "The bill is correct."

"What did you say?" asked Ludwig, who had taken out his purse and was carefully counting his money.

"The bill is right," said Fritz, a second time.

On the way home, they sat down to rest in a pasture where a flock of sheep was grazing. Violets made the air sweet with their fragrance. The sheep bleated softly. Their shepherd stood on a near-by hilltop. He raised a wooden pipe to his lips, and blew a long, soft call. It floated, pure and clear, through the stillness of the countryside.

"How sweet the shepherd's pipe sounds," said Fritz softly.

"Eh?" said Ludwig.

Fritz repeated what he had said.

"What shepherd? What pipe?" asked Ludwig, startled.

Fritz pointed. Ludwig saw the man's figure etched against the sky. He saw the pipe at the man's lips. But he heard nothing. He stood up and strained his ears. Nothing! He turned pale. He tried to speak, but no words came.

"Master, are you ill?" asked Fritz anxiously. Ludwig did not reply. Fritz guessed at once what was wrong. He saw that Ludwig could not hear the sound. He had noticed that Ludwig often failed to catch what was said to him.

"I can't hear the shepherd's pipe any more either," said Fritz, trying to comfort Ludwig.

But Ludwig only shook his head. The thing that he had feared had come to pass. For three years he had kept his trouble secret. At first there had been a buzzing in his ears. The buzzing was there only sometimes. It grew worse when he was tired. When it was bad, he could not understand what his friends said to him. They thought he was absent-minded; they did not know what was wrong, and he dared not tell them.

He had told his trouble to only two men. One was Dr. Wegeler, his boyhood friend from Bonn. The other was Karl Amenda, a young violinist whom he had met in Vienna five years before. His friendship with the gentle Amenda meant a great deal to him. Amenda had been playing the violin in a string quartet one evening when he had looked up to see the great Beethoven standing beside him, and had almost dropped his fiddle.

But Ludwig had praised his playing, and asked him to walk home with him after the music. They had played sonatas together in Ludwig's room and had talked for a while. Then Ludwig had proposed walking Amenda home to keep him company. In this way, they had walked back and forth all night long. After this, they had become close friends.

To Amenda, Ludwig had written a long letter confiding to him that he was losing his "noblest faculty," his hearing. That same year, he had written to his friend Dr. Wegeler: "For the last three years, my hearing has grown steadily worse. In the theater I must get very close to the orchestra in order to understand the actors. If I am a little distant, I do not hear the high tones of the instruments and singers, and if I am but a little farther away, I do not hear at all."

At last, his hearing had become so bad that he had consulted a doctor. "I am a musician," he said. "I *must* hear! Doctor, help me!"

"It is all a part of your stomach trouble," the doctor had said soothingly. "I will treat that first."

The doctor had tried, but he had not succeeded. Other doctors were called. They had given Ludwig cold baths, powders and pills. They had poured herbs and oils into his patient ears. But the buzzing continued.

Then a new doctor had advised, "Go to the country. Be alone for a few months. Give your ears a rest." On this advice, Ludwig had gone to Heiligenstadt that spring.

While walking with Fritz, he had forgotten his trouble. But now it struck him full force. He could not hear the shepherd's pipe!

For Ludwig, the sun shone no more that day. The flowers lost their scent. The sight of birds in flight reminded him that he could not hear their song. "How much longer can I keep my affliction secret? When people know that I am deaf, will they be willing to listen to my music?" he asked himself in agony. "A deaf composer! Surely I am the most miserable of men."

He did not take out his notebook on the way home. He did not sing. He did not talk. At his own door, he told Fritz, "I cannot give you a lesson." His voice was harsh with pain. Fritz went away silently, not daring even to say, "I am sorry."

In his own room, Ludwig raged up and down all night long, sometimes crying aloud in his pain and despair. At last, exhausted, he threw himself on his bed.

"I must make a plan," he cried. "I must! The doctors have not helped me. I must help

myself. I will stay in Heiligenstadt, alone."
After coming to this decision, he fell asleep.

Day after day, from May to October, he
tramped the green countryside. Most of the
time he was alone, but not entirely so, for music was always with him.

During the summer, he made sketches for
many piano pieces, and for the sunny, peace-
ful *Second Symphony*. Nobody, hearing this
music, would believe that the man who composed it was in the deepest despair.

But at summer's end, he set down his true
feelings in a long, sad letter to his brothers,
Karl and Johann, who were living in Vienna.
The letter was his last will and testament. It
is known as the Heiligenstadt Testament.

Ludwig did not mail it. He sealed it, and
locked it away in his desk. It was never opened
until he died, twenty-five years later. It is a
very precious paper, for it explains why Ludwig behaved as he did. He suffered so greatly
that he wished to die.

Yet, when he returned to Vienna, in October of 1802, the pages of his notebook were
covered with music. He wrote bravely to
Wegeler: "I will take Fate by the throat; it
shall not overcome me." He was going to
fight.

CHAPTER TWELVE

Symphony for a Hero

WHEN Ludwig came back to Vienna, he found everybody talking about Napoleon Bonaparte, the greatest figure in France. Napoleon had won many battles for France. He had established a bank and a new code of laws. He had recently been elected First Consul of France. He was a national hero. Wherever Napoleon appeared, crowds cheered him, bands played, and the French tricolor flag fluttered proudly.

"Long live Napoleon!" shouted the French people.

Napoleon was not an aristocrat. He was a man of the people. All the more, then, they loved every inch of his five feet. They loved his shiny military boots, his olive-green coat and white trousers, his two-cornered hat with its tricolor cockade. With the Revolution, the French working people had freed themselves from the tyranny of the nobles. Now they looked to Napoleon to keep them free.

To Ludwig, too, Napoleon appeared to be helping the French people to Liberty, Equality, and Brotherhood. Ludwig admired Napoleon. He saw himself, Ludwig van Beethoven, as the Napoleon of music. He would set it free from the old-time rules that hampered it. He would make new rules when the old ones did not suit his purpose. He intended to express in sound, in his own original way, men's deepest thoughts and feelings. He felt sure that he alone had the power to lead music to freedom of expression, as Napoleon alone had the power to lead the French people to political freedom.

He moved to new rooms, high up on the top floor of a house in the heart of Vienna. From his window, he could look over the whole city and feel like a Napoleon, free and powerful. He determined to write a third symphony, a Symphony to a Hero, and to dedicate it to Napoleon.

One evening, after a long walk, he found himself at the Swan Inn. He often met his friends there for dinner. He sat down by him-

self at a corner table and took out his notebook. Spreading a large sheet of paper under
the candle, he began to write music.

The waiter tiptoed to the table for his order, but he went away again. He knew Ludwig. He did not dare to disturb him.

For two hours, Ludwig sat at the table, his
lips moving silently, his pencil writing busily,

his eyes on the paper. Then he straightened
up, and rapped loudly on the table.

"Waiter!" he called. "My bill."

The waiter came running.

"But you have eaten nothing, sir," he said.

Ludwig uttered a great roar of laughter. He
looked around to see if others laughed too.

At the long table where he often ate with his friends, he spied Stephan von Breuning, "Falstaff" Schuppanzigh, and a few others. He went over to their table.

"We have been waiting for you," said Stephan. "Come on. Let's eat."

Ludwig took the seat they had saved for him at the head of the table. He patted his stomach with the palm of his hand as he sat down. "Don't I sound empty?" he asked, with another roar of laughter.

"Bring me a large bowl of bread soup with ten fresh eggs in it, beaten well. Ten, mind you!" he told the waiter. The others ordered fish, chicken, and wine. The waiter hurried off.

They talked of Napoleon.

"Everyone is afraid," said Stephan. "People say that Napoleon will conquer Austria and make Vienna a French city. What do you think, Ludwig?"

At times, Ludwig heard quite well. But on certain days, he had to pretend that he heard better than he did. Now he caught only the name, Napoleon.

"Napoleon is a great man," he said. "He is the champion of the people. I too am a champion of the people."

He raised his glass. "I drink to Napoleon," he said, "and to my new symphony, which I shall dedicate to Napoleon."

They all joined in the toast.

"Will you show us your new symphony?" asked Falstaff.

With a wicked twinkle, Ludwig handed him the paper he had been writing on.

"Falstaff will sing it for you," he told the others.

Falstaff took the paper. He was used to Ludwig's bad manuscript. But Ludwig had used a carpenter's pencil, with soft lead. The notes were all smeary and run together. Many had been scratched out, for Ludwig kept changing what he had put down.

With a shake of the head, Falstaff handed it back.

"I can't make head or tail of it. It's nothing but one great scrawl," he said.

"Ha, I knew that, or I would never have shown it to you," said Ludwig, who thought this a great joke. He reached across the table, knocking over a glass, and thrust the paper, all crumpled up, into his coat pocket.

"You shall all hear it some day," he promised.

The rising sun next morning made him

[*113*]

think of his hero, Napoleon, whose sun was also rising. At the top of a fair sheet of paper on his desk, he wrote with a flourish:

Symphony No. III
The Bonaparte Symphony
by
Louis van Beethoven

(He was sometimes called Louis instead of Ludwig.)

For the main theme of his first movement, he made a melody like the trumpet call of a conquering hero. This is the way it sounds:

From now on, he worked at the symphony for some part of every day. But there were many other things that kept him from finishing it.

He had promised to write an oratorio, *The Mount of Olives,* a big work for solo voices, chorus, orchestra, and organ, to be ready for a concert in April.

He had to correct the proofs of his music when the publishers sent them to him, however busy he was. "Errors swarm like fish in the sea," he complained, as he showed the publishers the many places he had to correct.

He was obliged to go to parties, although

the chattering voices and the loud laughter made his poor ears buzz frightfully. Go he did, for he could not offend the friends who loved him and his music.

It was a whole year before the *Hero Symphony* was finished. Meanwhile the score lay on Ludwig's writing table, on top of the scattered sheets of other unfinished works. Dull quill pens thick with ink, soiled handkerchiefs, plates of half-eaten food were on the writing table too. Ludwig never learned to be tidy. The older he grew, the more careless he became. He even spilled ink into his precious piano, if he happened to knock over the inkwell, waving his arms in the air while he composed.

One day in May, 1804, young Fritz Ries came to see him. Ludwig was shaving. His face from chin to forehead was covered with lather. When Fritz pounded on his door, Ludwig went, all lathered as he was, to open it.

"Fritz! Come in, come in!" Ludwig put down his razor and caught Fritz in his arms in a mighty bear-hug. The soapy white lather from his face went all over Fritz's. This was the kind of joke Ludwig liked.

"Ha-ha-ha!" he roared.

Fritz had to laugh too, though he felt foolish. He wiped his face, and sat down while Ludwig finished shaving.

"Have you heard the latest about Napoleon?" Fritz shouted after a while.

"Eh?" said Ludwig, cupping his hand over his ear.

"Napoleon," said Fritz, louder.

"What about Napoleon?" asked Ludwig.

"He has had himself crowned Napoleon the First, Emperor of the French," replied Fritz.

"What! Say that again!" cried Ludwig, throwing down the towel with which he was wiping his face. He thought he had not heard aright. Fritz repeated, and added, "They say that, at his coronation, he took the crown from the Pope's hand and himself set it on his own head."

"I cannot believe it!" cried Ludwig. "Do you mean to tell me that Napoleon is an ordinary man no different from other men? That he thinks only of his own ambition? That he will set himself above the people, and become a tyrant? Napoleon!"

He stamped over to the table where his *Third Symphony* lay. He seized the title page and tore it in half in a fury. He crumpled the halves and threw them on the floor.

"I will finish the symphony," he told Fritz. "But it shall not be dedicated to Napoleon.

I will dedicate it, instead, to His Serene Highness, Prince Lobkowitz."

In July, 1804, the finished score lay on his desk. The title page read: "Sinfonia Eroica, Composed to Celebrate the Memory of a Great Man."

The *Eroica* was strong and sure, original and powerful. It told in sweeping sound about his struggle to conquer his deafness, about his suffering, and finally about his victory. It is full of hope and courage. It is a symphony for a hero. But Beethoven himself was the hero whose memory the *Eroica* truly celebrates.

CHAPTER THIRTEEN

Ludwig's Only Opera

IT WAS a warm day in September. Ludwig, puffing his pipe, sat in a chair that was too small for his broad body, on the darkened stage of the Theater an der Wien. With him were Baron Braun, director of the theater, and blustery Herr Schikaneder, producer of operas. They had asked him to write the music for an opera. He was working on the *Eroica Symphony,* but the offer tempted him. He enjoyed writing several things at once. And besides, he had never tried his hand at an opera.

Herr Schikaneder had brought with him the story of a play called *Leonore.*

"Will you read this aloud, Herr Beethoven?" he asked. He feared that Ludwig might not hear well if it was read to him. Ludwig nodded, laid down his pipe, put on his spectacles, and took the book. In his loud, harsh voice, he read:

"Once upon a time there lived in ancient Spain a noble gentleman named Florestan, and his wife Leonore. They were good and gentle people. Pizarro, the head of the state, was their enemy. He was cruel and treated the townspeople unjustly. Pizarro had Florestan arrested and cast into prison on a false charge. Florestan's friends thought that he was dead. But his wife Leonore refused to believe that this was so. 'I will find my husband wherever he is!' she vowed.

"She put on boy's clothing because a highborn lady could not go about Spain alone. She took a boy's name, Fidelio, and went from prison to prison seeking Florestan. The pretty daughter of Rocco, head jailor of the largest prison, fell in love with the supposed boy. She persuaded her father to let Fidelio help carry food to the prisoners' cells.

"One day, Rocco told Fidelio that there was one prisoner in a deep dungeon they had not visited. Pizarro intended to kill him. He had been there for two years and was half dead already. 'Two years!' exclaimed Fidelio. And to herself, 'Alas, it is he!'

"Rocco had been ordered to dig a grave in

"Together they went to the underground dungeon"

the secret dungeon before Pizarro came to kill the prisoner. 'Take me down there with you,' begged Fidelio. 'I am young and strong. I can help to dig.' In that way, she hoped to see Florestan at least once more. 'Well—it is forbidden—but since it is for the last time—the poor fellow—yes,' said Rocco.

"Together they went to the underground dungeon. There lay the prisoner, chained to the flat stone that was his bed. 'It is Florestan, my husband,' murmured Fidelio to herself. 'I must find a way to save him.' While Rocco dug the grave, she gave the half-starved prisoner bread and wine, and urged him to have courage. In the dim light, he did not know who she was.

"The wicked Pizarro crept in, holding up his long, black cloak to hide his face. With gleaming knife held high, he approached the helpless prisoner. As he was about to plunge the knife into Florestan, Fidelio threw herself between them.

" 'I am Leonore, his wife!' she cried. 'You will have to kill me first!' Florestan, Pizarro, and Rocco were all struck dumb with amazement. Just then, a trumpet call sounded loud and clear. The governor, Florestan's friend, had come to visit the prison. Florestan was

[*121*]

saved. He owed his life to the faith and courage and love of a woman, his wife Leonore."

Ludwig closed the book.

"Ha, what a woman!" he exclaimed, clearing his throat and blowing his nose. "Such a woman as this I have never known. Such a woman as this I could marry."

"You cannot marry Leonore," said Schikaneder. "But," he added craftily, "you might write an opera about her. How do you like the story?"

"The story? It is a story of a man set free, is it not? Of course I like the story."

"What do you say, Baron?" asked Schikaneder.

Baron Braun saw how deeply Ludwig was moved.

"We do want an opera from you, Beethoven," he said quietly. "And this is a noble tale."

"Yes," said Ludwig. "I've had thirteen stories sent to me. But this is the one that really sings to me. To such a story as this, I can write music." So it was settled.

Baron Braun invited Ludwig to live in the Theater an der Wien while he was writing the opera. He accepted. But he kept his own lodgings besides. Sometimes he worked in the little room above the stage, heavy with the smell of grease paint and powder.

More often, he trotted through the streets, a strange figure in his bright blue coat with brass buttons and coattails flying. A colored handkerchief trailed from one of his pockets almost to the ground, and the other pockets

were stuffed with notebooks, paper, and pencils. On these walks, he looked neither to the right nor to the left, but up at the sky or down at the ground.

Sometimes he walked in the green park of the Emperor's palace of Schönbrunn, or

BEETHOVEN

settled in the crotch of a tree there, writing, erasing, creating, destroying.

When spring came, he hurried off to the country. "Nobody loves the country as I do. For it is forests, trees, and rocks that provide men with the resonance they desire," he wrote in his notebook. A few years later, he expressed that love in the *Sixth*, the *Pastoral Symphony*. Now, in the calm beauty of the hills and fields, he finished his opera.

In the early fall, he carried the heavy score of three long acts to Baron Braun.

With the *Eroica*, he had won the first round of the battle with his enemy, deafness. *Fidelio* marked the second round. His only opera! He had poured himself into it with all his heart and soul. How proud and happy he was that it was finished!

But now that Napoleon was Emperor, he wished to conquer Europe, as Ludwig had feared he would. His armies were marching into the towns around Vienna. Napoleon allowed his soldiers to plunder the cities they occupied. So the Empress, the Archduke Rudolph, Prince and Princess Lichnowsky, and all the nobles and bankers and wealthy music-lovers who could, fled from Vienna. They took with them their money and jewels and whatever else they could carry, to keep them from falling into the hands of the French.

Then rehearsals started. But the tenor who was to sing Florestan was drafted into the Austrian army. So, too, were many of the members of the orchestra.

Ludwig had marked on the score of *Fidelio* every *loud* and *soft,* every increase and decrease in sound, as he wished it sung. But he knew it could not succeed unless singers and orchestra were carefully rehearsed. And how was that possible, when every day he had newcomers with whom he had to start all over again?

One day, only two bassoon players came to the rehearsal. There should have been three. The bassoon has a deep, heavy sound. It was important that the third man should be there.

"Where is the third bassoon?" cried Ludwig.

"The first and second are here," said Prince Lobkowitz, who came to all the rehearsals. "What's the difference? Can't you get along without the third?"

The prince was trying to calm Ludwig, but he only made him angrier. On the way home after the rehearsal, Ludwig went by the prince's palace, with the Lobkowitz crest above its iron gates. He thrust his head in at the gates.

"Ass of a Lobkowitz!" he shouted.

The prince's servants thought Ludwig out of his mind to speak so of a nobleman. But the prince himself knew that sometimes Ludwig could not control his anger, and respected Ludwig's genius too much to be angry in his turn.

On November 15th, the victorious French army marched into Vienna with flags flying.

Five days later, the first performance of *Fidelio* was given. What a time to present a new German opera!

Napoleon was occupying the Austrian Emperor's palace of Schönbrunn. He did not attend the opera, but many of his officers did. Ludwig would have heard only French spoken, if he could have heard. For once, he preferred not to hear, tried not even to see the spick-and-span white trousers, blue coats, and glittering decorations of the French officers. He sat at the piano and conducted the performance—a little, dark, young-looking man with spectacles.

The French officers clapped their white-gloved hands politely. But they did not understand the words of the opera. They did not appreciate Ludwig's glorious music. They thought *Fidelio* much too long. They were bored. It was given only three times.

In due time, the French moved on to fresh conquests. Then the Empress and nobles ventured to return to Vienna. Ludwig's friend, Prince Lichnowsky, was especially eager to hear the opera. So was his princess, who had been very ill.

"We will invite the singers to come for an evening. We will ask Ludwig to bring the score. I will play the piano part," said the princess. "I am told that the opera is too long and should be shortened before it is given again. Perhaps we can persuade Ludwig to change it."

"If anyone can, you can, my dear," said the prince gallantly.

When Ludwig received his invitation to come and bring the score, he at once replied, "Natürlich, Ja. For the princess, I will come."

At noon of a cold December day, Ludwig sat in the Lichnowsky salon, score spread out on his knees. The princess, frail and wan, was at the piano. When the singers had arrived, and the violinist was in his place, Ludwig placed the score on the rack before the princess. She must have been a good musician indeed to play the score on the piano, at sight, from the orchestral score, especially with the composer listening!

When the first two acts were finished, all agreed that they were too long. All, that is, except Ludwig.

"Too long, you say! Not a note, not a note will I leave out!" he cried. He was offended. He tried to take his score from the piano. But the princess looked at him so pleadingly as she gently lifted his hands from the page that he sat down again. The tenor sang Florestan's aria, *In des Lebens Frühlingstagen* (*In the Springtime of Life*), which was Ludwig's favorite.

"Sing that again," said Ludwig, smiling. "Yet again," he commanded, beaming.

They worked all afternoon and evening, yet it was midnight before the whole opera had been played to the end.

"You will make the opera shorter?" asked the princess weakly. She looked so tired!

"No! Do not insist," said Ludwig. "No! Not a single note must be missing." He set his jaw stubbornly.

"Beethoven!" she implored. "Please give in! Please shorten the opera! You must! Your mother's spirit pleads with you through me. Do this in memory of your mother, do this for me, your truest friend!" She took his hand in hers. "Please!"

Ludwig was silent. Then he kissed her hand. The stubborn look left his face. He remembered his mother with tenderness.

"I will—yes, I will—for your—for my mother's sake," he whispered softly.

Everyone breathed a sigh of relief. They trooped into the dining room, and ate with good appetites the midnight supper the princess had provided. The talk was loud and merry. But Ludwig was silent and ate little; he was thinking of the mother he had loved so dearly.

The *Fidelio* that was a huge success eight years later, the *Fidelio* that is sung in opera houses all over the world today, is the *Fidelio* which Ludwig changed for his mother's sake.

"Of all my children, *Fidelio* is the one that brought me the most sorrow," said Ludwig, "and for that reason it is the one most dear to me."

CHAPTER FOURTEEN
Hard Times

LUDWIG had not heard the last of Napoleon. For in 1809, five years after the first performance of *Fidelio,* the French armies again attacked Vienna. Ludwig's servant came hammering at his door. It was nine o'clock in the evening.

"The French!" he cried. "Herr Beethoven, can you hear me? The French are attacking."

Ludwig was working, as usual. He had not noticed the distant boom of cannon. He heard only faintly what the man said.

"It's Napoleon! Napoleon, I say!" yelled the servant.

"What? Napoleon again? Bah! Close the shutters."

Ludwig stayed at his desk. But the booming came closer. His room was near the very wall that the French armies had chosen to attack. At last the noise became so loud that his poor ears could not stand it.

"I will go to my brother Karl in the center of town," he said. He often talked to himself, he was so much alone.

As he hurried through the dark streets, he saw wounded men and weeping women. Lost children wandered about, seeking their parents. Ludwig's anger against the French burned hot. He shook his fist in the air.

"If I, as a general, knew as much about the art of war as I, as a composer, know about the art of music, I'd give the French something to worry about," was his greeting to his brother when Karl opened the door.

"Come in, come in," said Karl, who saw how upset his brother was.

"What a wild, desolate life around me!" mourned Ludwig as he stepped across the threshold. "Nothing but drums, cannon, misery."

"Come, you will be comfortable in my cellar," said Karl. He lighted Ludwig down the narrow stairs with a candle. He brought pillows and blankets, and a pot of coffee.

Ludwig buried his head in the pillows. He covered his ears with the blankets. He did not come out of the cellar for two days and three nights. He was not afraid, but he could not bear the noise.

On May 12, the Austrian army raised the white flag of truce. For the second time, the French army occupied Vienna. They had been there when *Fidelio* was first performed. Now, there they were again. It seemed that Napoleon had made up his mind that the lovely city of Vienna *must* be his.

It was spring, and Ludwig longed to go to the country as usual. But the French permitted no one to leave the city. They closed the Prater and the gardens of Schönbrunn, where Ludwig loved to walk.

In July, a great battle was fought, and Napoleon's armies were beaten by the Austrians. But it was not until December that a peace treaty was signed. The hated French flag flew above Vienna all summer.

This was very hard on Ludwig. For the first time in quite a while, he needed money. Austrian paper florins were now worth almost nothing because of the French occupation. And he could not turn for help to his wealthy friends. They all had fled at the first report that the French were coming again into Austria.

He particularly missed Prince Rasumowsky, the Russian ambassador to Austria. Ludwig had spent many happy hours in the prince's magnificent palace in the country. He had written three "Rasumowsky" quartets to the prince's order, and the prince had paid him well, and had given him two bronze statues of Russian Cossacks as a keepsake. Ludwig kept them on his desk and used them as bookends.

Ludwig greatly missed three other good friends, Prince Lobkowitz, Prince Kinsky, and the Archduke Rudolph. These men had agreed to give Ludwig a certain sum of money every year, to help him pay his bills. This

agreement had been made because of something which had happened a year earlier.

Ludwig had returned to his room in Vienna from the Rasumowsky palace one day, to find a messenger in royal livery at his door.

"I am looking for Herr Ludwig van Beethoven," said the man.

"I am Beethoven," said Ludwig simply.

"My master, King Jerome Napoleon Bonaparte of Westphalia, sent me, sir." The man took off his hat and bowed respectfully.

At the name of Bonaparte, Ludwig became very attentive. What could Napoleon's young brother want from him?

"My master invites you to be his court musician," said the man. "If you will come to

Cassel he will give you six hundred gold ducats a year and your traveling expenses."

Ludwig was tempted. He was flattered, too.

"I must have time to think," he replied. "Come back next week for my answer."

Of course, he told his friends about the offer the very first chance he had.

"The people of Vienna do not appreciate my music," he said. "The Emperor does not, either. Why, by this time I ought to be Imperial Conductor, at the very least. Perhaps I should accept the offer to go to Cassel."

"We will not let you go!" cried the Archduke Rudolph, Prince Kinsky, and Prince Lobkowitz. "We will pay you the same amount in Austrian paper florins as King Bonaparte has offered to pay you in ducats, if you will stay here."

Because Ludwig did not really want to go to Cassel, a small German city; because he loved Vienna; because he loved his friends, he had agreed to stay.

But now his friends' paper florins were worth nothing. And everything cost twice as much as usual. Food was scarce and poor. Ludwig was very worried.

To make matters worse, he became ill. He had had trouble with his stomach for many years. Poor food now made his trouble worse. He was always taking some kind of medicine for his stomach and his deafness. But he had his own way of taking medicine. Sometimes he would swallow in one dose all the six different kinds of pills and powders that he was supposed to take in the course of the day. Sometimes he would drink his medicine from the bottle without measuring it. No wonder it did him no good.

Yet, during the French occupation, he worked and worked and worked. He wrote a piano sonata for the Archduke, in three parts

—*Farewell, Absence,* and *Return,* because his friend had left the city, was away for a time, then came back again. He wrote a noble piano concerto, the *Emperor Concerto.* He composed a string quartet.

He prepared his *Fourth, Fifth,* and *Sixth Symphonies* and his only violin concerto for the publisher; all were printed this year. And he wrote other works besides. Napoleon and all his armies could not silence Ludwig's voice. Neither could ill health, deafness, or poverty. When his friends returned to Vienna, he was waiting for them with his radiant smile, with wide-open arms, and with a pile of music they must hear. This was the great Beethoven, the man they loved.

CHAPTER FIFTEEN

Metronome Symphony

E<small>H?</small> Speak louder."

Ludwig directed his ear trumpet to the speaker at his right at the dinner table. He was dining with friends at an outdoor café. It was a soft evening in May, 1812. The next day, he was to go away to take a cure for the stomach-aches that troubled him. This was his farewell party.

The speaker was Johann Mälzel, an inventor. Mälzel had started telling Ludwig about all the newest inventions. Stephan von Breuning, the Count von Brunswick, and one or two others were listening.

"Bring on the dinner," called Ludwig loudly. "Eat, drink, and be merry, everybody!"

He was in what he called his "unbuttoned"

mood, happy and free from care. How he enjoyed his food! Soup, fish, Wiener Schnitzel with paprika noodles, and Vienna pastry with gobs of whipped cream. He took two pastries.

When the coffee was brought in, Ludwig unbuttoned his vest, and looked around for a toothpick. Mälzel handed him one made from a goose quill.

"Try this," he said. "I made it myself."

"It is like the goose-quill pens one of my friends sharpens for me," said Ludwig as he took it. "I can't sharpen them myself. I cut my fingers when I try."

"Have you seen the new fillable pen?" shouted Mälzel. "It is filled with ink and carried about in the pocket. No goose quill to sharpen."

"Where can I get one?" asked Ludwig quickly. "Perhaps if I have one I won't keep upsetting my inkwell." Mälzel gave him the name of the goldsmith who manufactured the grandfather of the fountain pen.

"I've heard of another remarkable invention," said Mälzel, "a boat that goes by steam. No sails are necessary."

"Heavens!" exclaimed Ludwig.

"I believe they are working on a steam cannon too," Mälzel said.

"Let us thank God for the promised steam cannon and the already realized steam navigation," said Ludwig solemnly.

"A jeweler in Vienna is trying to build a flying machine," added Mälzel, enjoying the effect of his words on the company.

"Crazy!" they exclaimed with one voice.

"My own invention is not a flying machine," Mälzel assured them. "It is more practical."

"What is it? An ear trumpet?" asked Ludwig hopefully.

"No, sir. I will make you an ear trumpet if you wish," replied Mälzel. "But this is something I call a chronometer."

"Isn't that a fancy name for a clock?" asked Stephan.

"Yes, but this is no clock, though it beats time like a clock. It is made especially for musicians. It beats even, regular beats, fast or slow, according to the way one sets it."

"Ha! The orchestra won't need a conductor then. Ludwig, you will be out of a job," teased Stephan.

"Oh, yes, conductors will use my chronometer," said Mälzel. "For the composer will write above his music a number which will tell the conductor how fast or slow the machine should be set to play the piece at the correct speed. Do you all understand?"

"But this is wonderful!" said Ludwig. "Have you brought one with you? Or is it too big to carry?"

For answer, Mälzel reached into his pocket. He placed a small, square box on the table. He started the machinery.

"*Tick-tock. Tick-tock.*" A little hammer on a lever released by a cog-wheel tapped slowly and steadily on a wooden anvil.

"Can it go faster?" asked Ludwig. He was really interested.

Mälzel pushed something. Now the little hammer beat fast and merrily—"*Tick-tock, tick-tock, tick-tock.*"

"What a machine!" roared Ludwig. He played with it, making it go faster, slower, faster. He watched it closely, for he could hear the ticking only faintly, if indeed he heard it at all.

"Your chronometer makes me think of a tune!" he exclaimed, when he had set it very fast. And he sang:

ta-ta   ta ta-ta ta ta-ta Ta ta   ta ta-ta-ta ta ta-ta ta

"I'll write words," Stephan offered. And to Ludwig's tune he sang:

"Farewell, farewell, farewell,
My very goo-ood friend, Mä-alzel."

"All sing!" cried Ludwig gaily. He seized a fork and beat on the table. The machine ticked in time with his beat. He sang a harsh tenor. Mälzel growled a rough bass. The others joined in as best they could. They sounded so merry that the landlord and his wife came to see what was going on, and remained to sing along.

The party broke up late. As soon as the others had gone, Ludwig put down the "ta-ta-ta" melody in his notebook.

After a time, a pendulum and weight were substituted for the hammer and anvil, a triangular box took the place of the square one, and the name *chronometer* was changed to *metronome*.

The day after the supper party, the postilion's horn called Ludwig early to take the coach for Teplitz. Teplitz was a health resort. In Teplitz, he took the baths and drank the bitter waters that his doctor said would cure him. In Teplitz, he finished the *Seventh Symphony*, and started the *Eighth*.

"Ta-ta-ta, ta-ta-ta, ta-ta-ta," he hummed. He used the metronome melody in the laughing third movement of the *Eighth Symphony*. Because of this, the *Eighth* is called the *Metronome Symphony*.

In Teplitz, Ludwig met the German poet, Goethe. Ludwig admired Goethe's poetry, Goethe admired Ludwig's music. But the two men were very different. Goethe was quiet, elegant, and polite. Ludwig spoke his mind loudly and freely.

Yet, for a time, he and Goethe saw each

other quite often. The two men were walking arm in arm down the street one morning. Many people bowed as they passed.

"It's a nuisance to greet so many people," Goethe complained. Of course, he did not really mean this; he was flattered that everyone knew him.

"Don't let that trouble Your Excellency," said Ludwig mischievously. "Perhaps the greetings are intended for *me.*"

They continued walking. In the distance, they saw the Empress, the Archduke, and the whole glittering court approaching.

"Her Majesty the Empress!" exclaimed Goethe. He took off his hat and started to move to one side of the narrow street to let them pass.

"Stay where you are!" commanded Ludwig. "They must make way for us, not we for them. We are artists. They are only royalty."

Goethe let go of Ludwig's arm nevertheless, and stepped aside. Hat in hand, he bowed humbly.

Ludwig stood where he was, head held high. The royal party bowed and smiled. They divided where he stood, and flowed past him on both sides. Not until then did Ludwig take off his hat. When Goethe returned, Ludwig reproved him.

"I waited for you, because I honor and respect you, but you did those dressed-up people too much honor," he said. "You have lived too much in the atmosphere of courts, more than a poet should."

Ludwig, too, had lived in the atmosphere of courts. But he had remained a man of the people. Now the people were to know his music better. For he was about to produce what we would call today a "best seller."

CHAPTER SIXTEEN
Best Seller

A YEAR after the supper party, Mälzel
made Ludwig the promised ear trumpet, and
brought it to his room.

"It works no better than any of the others,"
grumbled Ludwig, throwing it on the bench
where half a dozen already lay.

"Come and see my other inventions," proposed Mälzel, to make him forget his disap-
pointment.

At Mälzel's exhibit, Ludwig stood in amazement before a mechanical chess player, and a
mechanical trumpeter who raised a shaky
trumpet to his lips and played military
marches. He lingered long before the Panharmonicon.

This was a machine that played all the instruments of a military band. They were
blown with a bellows. Pins on a revolving

brass cylinder touched their keys to make the
tune. Bellows, instruments, and cylinder
were all in a glass case. The whole machine
looked like the old-fashioned music boxes we
sometimes see in museums. It was such a
curiosity that people were willing to pay ad-
mission just to look at it.

"Wunderbar!" cried Ludwig, as excited as
a boy. Mälzel played for him on the Panharmonicon a military march by Haydn and an
overture by Handel, two famous composers.

"Will you write a piece for the Panharmonicon, Herr Beethoven?" Mälzel was bold
enough to ask.

"What will you do with it?" asked Ludwig.

"I will take it to England. I am going to give concerts there with the mechanical trumpeter and Panharmonicon. Will you come along? We can make money."

It was a daring thing to ask the great Beethoven to write music for a machine. But Ludwig did not say no. Mälzel saw that he rather liked the idea.

"How about writing a military march?" Mälzel asked, "to celebrate General Wellington's victory over Napoleon's army at the Battle of Vittoria in Spain? The English would like that, since Wellington is a British general."

"Napoleon again!" exclaimed Ludwig. "Yes! I'll do it! We will call the march *Wellington's Victory*."

It took him only a short time to compose *Wellington's Victory*. The march tells in music the whole story of the battle. Two groups of wind instruments are the opposing armies. Bullets whistle in the piccolo. Cannon boom in the bass drums. Horses gallop to drum beats. The French and English armies march and countermarch to clashing cymbals and trumpet fanfares. The French sing their rousing song, "Malbrouck s'en va t'en guerre." After the battle is won, the English sing in triumph, "Rule, Britannia."

When the piece was all ready for the Panharmonicon, it struck Mälzel that they could make money toward their trip if they first gave the military march in Vienna. Ludwig agreed to arrange it for the orchestra.

"Let the trial performance be for charity," suggested Mälzel. So an "Academy" was arranged. Well-known musicians offered to play in the orchestra—"Falstaff" Schuppanzigh led the violins. Meyerbeer, a young opera composer, beat the bass drum. Moscheles, a pianist who greatly admired Ludwig, clashed the cymbals. Dragonetti played the double bass. Ludwig conducted. At the same concert, he introduced his *Seventh Symphony*.

The audience enjoyed so much seeing the many famous people on the stage that they paid hardly any attention to the glorious *Seventh Symphony*. But they took *Wellington's Victory* to their hearts. They clapped long and hard and shouted and called for more of the march. This was the only composition of Ludwig's, up to that time, that was received with so much excitement. It is far from his best. He despised the bad taste of the audience, but he enjoyed their applause.

After this, *Wellington's Victory* was performed again and again. Ludwig made more money with it than he had with all his symphonies. His name was on every tongue. A portrait of him was engraved and displayed in the shopwindows. He had a "best seller."

At this time, the kings and queens of Europe, the Empress of Russia, and important men from many countries were assembled in Vienna. They had come together to decide what was to be done about Napoleon. The French Emperor had tried on many battlefields to make himself the ruler of Europe. But now he had been beaten in Russia, had been taken prisoner, and was being held on the island of Elba. He had not yet been finally defeated at Waterloo.

The Congress of Vienna, as the brilliant gathering was called, was in no hurry to talk about the French Emperor.

"The business of Napoleon can wait. Later, we will restore the conquered countries to their rulers. Let us enjoy Vienna while we are here," they agreed. It was one of the few things they did agree on.

They went to balls and parties. They attended special performances of concerts and operas in their honor. Ludwig van Beethoven, the leading composer of Vienna, was on hand to help entertain them. He decided not to go to England with Mälzel; this was not the time for him to leave Vienna.

Prince Rasumowsky had a wing built on to his magnificent palace so that he could entertain seven hundred guests at a time. Ludwig went to all his parties, and to those that the Archduke Rudolph gave too. The famous Beethoven was the main attraction at these festivities. His friends, the princes, were proud to show him off.

The rulers of Europe showered gifts and money on him. He wrote a polonaise for the Empress of Russia. He composed a new cantata, *The Glorious Moment*.

For Ludwig, the year 1814 *was* a glorious moment in his life. He heard his opera *Fidelio* sixteen times that year, and every time the house was crowded. Both the royal visitors and the ordinary people came, six thousand strong, when Beethoven conducted his *Seventh* and *Eighth Symphonies,* and *The Glorious Moment,* in the largest hall in Vienna. "Bravo, Beethoven, bravo!" they cheered, as they clapped their gloved hands.

At the end of the concert, Ludwig bowed deeply. He walked to the piano and seated himself. The house was so quiet, you could have heard a pin drop. Not a fan fluttered. Beethoven never played the piano in public any more. He was too deaf to hear what he was playing. But now he improvised most beautifully. This was his way, the Beethoven way, of saying, "Thank you," to royalty. It was the last time he played the piano in public.

His forty-fourth year was the happiest in his life. It was the last happy year he was to know.

CHAPTER SEVENTEEN

Beethoven Adopts a Nephew

Fire! Fire!"

The cry broke out at a great party in Prince Rasumowsky's palace. Many of the nobles who attended the Congress of Vienna were there. So, too, was Beethoven.

The cry froze his blood. He shuddered as he recalled the awful night when he had first heard it, when the Elector's palace in Bonn had burned. He seemed again to hear the jangling bells as he watched helplessly while the tower fell. He again had to watch helplessly while flames devoured priceless treasures.

The guests escaped unharmed. So did the prince. So did Ludwig. But the rare instruments, the paintings and sculptures all went up in flames. This was Beethoven's New Year's Eve celebration on Dec. 31, 1814.

After this, the prince did not rebuild his

palace. He ordered no more quartets from Ludwig. But the fire could not destroy the three he had already written. They will live forever.

Eleven months after the fire, Beethoven had another piece of bad news. His brother Karl, the redhead, was very ill. Karl sent for Ludwig. As their mother had done long ago, he whispered, "Promise—promise me—take care of little Karl. I—will make—you—guardian."

Little Karl was Karl's only child. He was nine years old. Ludwig promised to care for him as if he were his own. Karl's mother was made part guardian. But Ludwig did not like her. He did not want to have anything to do with her. When big Karl died, little Karl was told that he must go to live with his Uncle Ludwig.

Beethoven was glad to have a little boy, someone to love, someone who would love him in return.

"You must become an artist or a scholar," he told the boy. "Only the artist and the scholar carry their happiness with them." Nine-year-old Karl looked at him with big eyes. He did not know what his uncle was talking about.

Beethoven was forty-five years old and unmarried. He did not know, as a father would, how to feed a little boy, how to educate him, how to make him happy, how to teach him to love him. Karl thought Uncle Ludwig was a very queer and cranky old bachelor.

For a time, Beethoven sent him to a boarding school, while he prepared his household to receive a little boy. But he, who could direct a symphony orchestra, could not direct a household. "My household greatly resembles a shipwreck, or threatens to," wailed Beethoven. And that is the way Karl found it when he arrived from boarding school with his chest of clothes.

Every morning, at breakfast, Karl watched his uncle count coffee beans. Gretchen, the servant, was ordered to put exactly sixty beans on his plate. With the sixty beans, Ludwig made his own coffee in a glass pot. One day, he counted only fifty-eight beans. Then there was an outcry. Beethoven lost his temper. "I am being robbed!" he cried, and threw a book at the girl's head. She ran out of the house and never came back. Karl wished he could do the same.

When Beethoven was composing, he would pour a pitcher of cold water over his head and hands to cool them. Karl, in the room below, would watch the water drip down from the ceiling. Nobody mopped it up. Much of the time, there was no servant to do so, or to cook a decent meal, or to clean the house.

Karl did not like his uncle's way of living. He did not like his uncle. He ran away to his mother. His uncle Ludwig brought him back, and told him how dearly he loved him, and begged for his love. But Karl ran away again. His mother tried to get him away from Beethoven. She went to the law court about it. The judge listened to her side of the story. He listened to Beethoven's.

When Beethoven came before the judge with his ear trumpet, the judge was very respectful. He knew what a great man Beethoven was. He asked, "Sir, is the *van* in your name a mark of your noble birth?"

"My nobility is here," said Beethoven, touching his heart, "and here," touching his head.

The judge was impressed. He heard all the arguments. He decided that Karl's mother was not a fit guardian. From now on, Beethoven and a man appointed by the court were to be Karl's only legal guardians. This was a victory for Beethoven. But it took three years to settle.

BEETHOVEN

When Beethoven was forty-seven, he received a wonderful present. It was a fine English piano. The Broadwood Company sent it all the way from London to the great Beethoven. He would allow no one but himself to touch it, even to tune it. But he gave Karl a lesson on it one day, as a special treat. Alas, he could not hear how his new Broadwood sounded. He no longer heard even when people shouted into his ear trumpet. They had to write what they said to him. Even Karl had to write on a slate his answers to the many questions his uncle asked.

"What did you do this morning? This afternoon? How many hours did you practice? Where did you go after school? Who was with you? How much money did you spend? What did you do with the pocket money I gave you?"

Karl hated to write the answers. He wished his uncle would let him alone. He often lied. The older he grew, the more often he lied.

He fell into bad habits. He wasted his time when he should have been studying. He played truant from school. He gambled at cards and lost. He borrowed, and played again. When he was very hard up, he borrowed from Beethoven's cashbox without even asking.

Of course he did not dare tell his troubles to his excitable uncle. The older and deafer Beethoven grew, the harder it was to tell him anything. And the older Karl grew, the more there was to tell. It was worst when Karl asked for money. They quarreled. They made up. They quarreled again. They had a miserable time.

Yet, during the years while Karl was growing up, from 1815 to 1824, Beethoven composed two of his very grandest works. One was the *Missa Solemnis,* a solemn mass to honor the Archduke Rudolph when he became an archbishop. The other was the *Ninth Symphony.*

This was the very first symphony in all of music, in which voices, as well as instruments, took part. The last movement has a tremendous chorus and soloists singing with the orchestra. The *Ninth* is called the *Choral Symphony* for this reason. Ludwig put into these works the big, beautiful thoughts he had thought all his life long.

Karl often listened at the door while his uncle worked. Often Beethoven roared aloud and stamped about as if he were in pain. Sometimes he rushed, without hat or coat, into the street, seeing nothing and nobody, and did not return for many hours. Other times, he locked himself in and did not come out, even to eat, till Karl had given up hope.

But at last he could say, "My work is finished."

At last he could announce:

A GRAND MUSICAL CONCERT

BY

Mr. L. van Beethoven

MAY 7, 1824

In the Hoftheater (Court Theater) beside the Kärtnerthor. Mr. Ludwig van Beethoven will himself direct.

On this great evening, Beethoven would again see some of the good friends he had not seen for many months. Prince Lichnowsky had died. Prince Rasumowsky had left Vienna.

The Archduke Rudolph was away. But a sick friend had declared he would have himself carried there in a sedan chair, rather than miss the concert. And there were many others who would be eager to hear him conduct the first performance of his *Ninth Symphony,* and a part of the *Missa Solemnis.*

It was the night of the concert, May 7, 1824. Beethoven was in his place at the conductor's stand in the center of the orchestra. His back was turned to the crowded house, his eyes were fixed on the score. He had to direct soloists, a chorus, and a symphony orchestra.

Sopranos, altos, tenors, and basses sang the choruses at the top of their lungs. Strings, woodwinds, brasses, and drums were scraped, blown, and beaten. The orchestra of Beethoven's day was only half the size it is today. Yet what a big sound they made, together with the singers!

Alas, Beethoven could not hear it. And since he could not, he had no way of telling the soloists when to come in. He could not know whether the chorus was singing loud or soft. Often he would be crouching low, as he did when he wished the sound to be soft, while at that very moment they were singing at the top of their lungs. Or he would be on tiptoes for a loud climax, when they had not yet reached it. The chorus sang a *Hymn to Joy.* But everyone felt sorry for Beethoven. They could see that now his hearing was completely gone, for he could not hear that tremendous rush of sound.

"Watch Beethoven, but do not follow his beat, follow mine," the assistant conductor had whispered to singers and players before the concert. He stood beside Beethoven, and struggled to hold the vast army of performers together. But the singers and the orchestra often lost one another. The sopranos sounded shrill, the chorus sang out of tune.

At such times, it was just as well that Ludwig could not hear what they were doing to his music. But then again, there were moments of such beauty that the audience burst into applause while the music was still going on. At the very end, there was a great roar of approval and a prolonged clapping. All eyes turned to Beethoven.

There he stood, still beating time! His imagination was filled with the beautiful sounds of the symphony which he had taken thirty years to write. Now he did not know that the performance had come to an end. He did not realize that the chorus was no longer singing. His eyes on the score, his back to the audience, he heard not a whisper of the applause. Poor Beethoven!

One of the singers pulled his sleeve. He looked up. She turned his shoulders gently so that he faced the audience. Now he could *see* the applause. There was even more than before. Tears poured down his cheeks as he bowed again and again. He took off his silver-rimmed spectacles and wiped his eyes.

By this time, everyone in the house was crying. They thought it very sad that such a great genius should not be able to hear the glorious music he had created. But what a victory for Beethoven, to create such music in spite of his deafness, in spite of his nephew, in spite of his ill health! At this moment, he felt that he was strong enough to face all these troubles, and to conquer them.

CHAPTER EIGHTEEN

House of the Black Spaniard

PAPA, Mamma, do you know that strange-looking man walking toward us? He seems to know you."

Young Gerhard von Breuning pointed to a stocky figure with an ear trumpet sticking out of the bulging blue coat pocket. Ludwig was crossing the cobblestoned square.

"Why, yes—it must be—it *is* my friend Beethoven!"

Stephan had not seen Ludwig for a long time. As Beethoven grew older and deafer, he cared less and less to see people, even old friends like Stephan von Breuning. Beethoven was now fifty-five.

"How he has changed!" exclaimed Stephan.

Beethoven's once black hair was iron gray.

A low top hat was pushed way back on his head. His legs in light trousers under the blue coat looked too short for his body. But his eyes lit up when he recognized Stephan.

The two men ran into each other's arms and embraced, both talking at once. Thirteen-year-old Gerhard, standing beside his mother, watched them with interest.

"Papa likes that man," he whispered to her. "I do, too. He looks queer, but nice. When he smiles, he looks kind."

Stephan tried to introduce his wife and son, shouting into the ear trumpet Beethoven extended to him. But Beethoven shook his head. "It's no use," he sighed. He patted Gerhard's rosy cheek gently, and handed him a book and pencil.

"Will you write whatever you have to say to me, my boy?" he asked. A strange way to converse on a street corner!

Beethoven started by asking Stephan questions. "Where do you live? How many children have you? How are our friends in Bonn? How is your work going?" he asked eagerly. Gerhard wrote the answers his father told him to.

"In a few days, I shall move into the House of the Black Spaniard," said Beethoven.

"The House of the Black Spaniard! That sounds scary!" said Gerhard, and wrote it.

"I looked like a black Spaniard myself when I was young, and the boys called me Spangy. Remember, Stephan?" asked Beethoven.

Stephan nodded.

"I remember. But this house is so called because the Spanish Benedictine monks who lived in it many years ago wore black robes," Stephan told Gerhard. "It is directly across the street from the Red House, where we live."

Gerhard scribbled excitedly, "We live across the street."

"So? Well then, dear good Frau von Breuning, will you arrange my household for me? I am alone. My nephew Karl lived with me while he was going to the University of

Vienna. But this fall, he changed to the Polytechnic Institute. Imagine! He wants to become a businessman, not an artist!" Beethoven shook his head sadly.

"Karl is living near the Institute," Beethoven continued. "A great worry, since I cannot watch him as carefully as I wish to. But usually he comes to me for week ends. Will you help me, Frau von Breuning? It is more difficult for me than for anyone else to set up a household, for I know nothing at all about such things, nothing."

Frau von Breuning was ready and willing to help her husband's old friend. She sent Gerhard to help, too. He ran errands. He unpacked. He hung Grandfather's portrait where Beethoven could see it from his bed. He helped arrange on Beethoven's desk the two bronze Cossacks which Prince Rasumowsky had given him, and which he still used as book ends. There was also a plaster bust of the Roman, Brutus, whom Beethoven admired as a champion of the people against tyranny. And a three-legged handbell with which he called his servant—when there was a servant to call.

Beside Beethoven's bed stood a small table. On this, Gerhard placed a black tin cashbox,

[*167*]

within easy reach of Beethoven's hand, a pencil and slate and conversation books. A folding desk on the other side of the bed held notebooks with sketches for a *Tenth Symphony,* ideas for a new opera, and other notes. Beethoven was ill very often these days, but he worked in bed, even when he felt sick and miserable.

He called Gerhard "Trouser-button."

"I couldn't get along without my Trouser-button, could I?" he often said, laughingly rumpling the boy's hair.

The child did for him the many things that Karl should have done, had he loved him as Gerhard did. Because Gerhard lived across the street, he could run in and out several times a day.

Karl came home sometimes on Saturdays and Sundays. He was now almost twenty. Beethoven continued to treat him as though he were ten.

Late one Saturday, Karl tiptoed into the house. He hoped that his uncle would be asleep. But Beethoven was waiting up for him.

"Come into my study," he called. "Where have you been?"

It took Karl a minute or two to reach for the conversation book.

"You've been with that fellow Niemetz again, haven't you?" asked his uncle.

Karl nodded, "Yes."

"Haven't I told you I do not like him?" stormed Beethoven.

Again Karl nodded, "Yes."

"He takes you to play billiards and makes you spend too much of my money," raged his uncle.

"He is my friend," wrote Karl.

"He is a low-down, good-for-nothing spend-thrift. I know all about him. I have inquired. You must not see him any more."

"I will so," retorted Karl, without bothering to write.

"I forbid it." Beethoven raised his voice.

"I will, I WILL!" Karl wrote in big, black letters.

"I will not allow him in my house!" shouted Beethoven.

Karl, so angry he did not know what to do next, raised his hand to strike his uncle.

"Karl!" Beethoven's sharp cry brought the young man to his senses. His fist unclenched. His hand fell to his side.

"I will kill myself," he said somberly—and wrote it.

Now his uncle was frightened. He told Karl

[*169*]

how much he loved him. He told him that he acted as he did for Karl's own good.

"Be my dear, only son," he begged. "Oh, do not grieve me further."

Karl listened sullenly. He pretended to be friends again, but he did not really feel friendly.

After this, Beethoven worried about him more than ever. They quarreled more than ever. Karl would not be seen on the street with his uncle. Little boys on street corners jeered at Beethoven's untidy figure as he forced his way with short, jerky steps through the bustling crowds. When people stood in his path, he brushed them aside. Often he would stop short, to ponder, to growl a melody, to write something down. Then the little boys stopped with him, imitating him.

"He's an old fool," Karl told his friend Niemetz. He did not know that love of him and worry about him were making his uncle behave as he did.

On a Saturday in July, 1826, Karl left the house, desperate after a terrible quarrel.

"I will disown you," Beethoven shouted after him.

"I will never come back," yelled Karl.

He was gone all night. He did not come

home the next morning. His uncle was frantic. He went to look for Karl, sent his friends searching, even begged Niemetz, Karl's "good-for-nothing" friend, for help.

Karl was found at last. A farmer spied the young man lying under a tree in a park which was one of his uncle's favorite spots. Beside Karl lay a pistol. He had shot himself. His head was bloody. He was unconscious.

"Thank God, it was a glancing shot! He lives, and there is hope he will be saved. But the disgrace he has brought upon me! And I loved him so!" Beethoven brokenly told Frau von Breuning when the news was brought to him.

The bullet had wounded Karl only slightly.

"Take me to my mother's house here in the city," he told the teamster who found him.

Beethoven rushed to his bedside.

"I can never trust you any more," he said. "How could you do this to me?"

Karl turned his face to the wall. When Beethoven had gone, Karl said to his mother: "If only he would stop reproaching me! If only he would not come here again! If you mention his name, I will tear off my bandage. I grew worse, because my uncle so wanted me to be better."

[*171*]

Karl was taken to a hospital. When the wound was healed, he would be arrested and sent to prison for trying to kill himself. This was the law in Vienna.

Ludwig could not bear the thought. The nephew of Ludwig van Beethoven would be treated no better than any common criminal! He went for advice to Stephan von Breuning.

"What shall I do?" he asked helplessly.

"Send Karl to the army," his friend advised. "Let him become a soldier. The army is a strict guardian. It will keep him out of mischief. If he is a soldier, I may be able to arrange with the police not to send him to prison."

"That suits me," said Karl, when his uncle told him of this plan. He was delighted to get away from Uncle Ludwig.

"But first you must be entirely well," said Beethoven. "I will ask your Uncle Johann if we may stay with him in the country."

Beethoven needed the country worse than Karl. All the excitement had made him really ill. He had grown very thin. He paid less attention than ever to the food he ate, or the clothes he wore, or the bed he slept in. At fifty-six, he looked like an old man of seventy-six.

But when he reached his brother's house in the country, he felt better. There he could be by himself much of the time. He wrote in his notebook, "I am never alone when I am alone."

He was not alone because music was again with him. He was composing a string quartet. One day, as he walked along the country road, singing and waving his arms, he came face to face with a man driving a team of oxen. The oxen were frightened by Beethoven's motions, and started to run away.

"Whoa!" cried their driver. "Be quiet, please!" he called to Beethoven.

Beethoven did not hear a word. He went right on waving his arms and singing. The

oxen bolted, and the driver had a hard time catching them.

"Who is that fool?" he gasped angrily, all out of breath, as he seized the oxen's yoke.

"That? Oh, that's Johann Beethoven's brother," replied a peasant who had stopped to give him a hand.

"A fine brother he is!" sneered the driver, patting his trembling animals. He did not know that Beethoven had heard not a word, that he was thinking so hard that he had not even seen the runaway oxen.

While Beethoven composed his string quartet, Karl enjoyed the lazy life in the country. He made friends with the pretty girls in the village. He hung around the village inn. He did not want to go back to the House of the Black Spaniard.

"The longer we are here, the longer we can be together. When we return to Vienna, I shall have to join my regiment. I shall have to leave you," he wrote on Ludwig's pad.

"Perhaps he loves me a little, after all," his uncle told himself hopefully. He had no idea that Karl was only pretending to love him, to induce him to stay longer in the country.

In September, Johann's wife drove back to Vienna in the closed carriage. Beethoven and

Karl stayed on with Johann. Beethoven and his brother had a bitter quarrel. Beethoven insisted that his brother should make a will, leaving all his money to Karl.

"I'll do nothing of the sort," Johann told him hotly. "It's no business of yours what I choose to do with my money."

They argued back and forth. After such a quarrel, Beethoven had no choice but to leave. Besides, it was December, the house was unheated and bitter cold. He sent Karl to the village to hire a carriage, for Johann's was in Vienna. All that Karl could find was an open carriage. An open carriage, in December!

They left on a freezing cold day. Beethoven shivered in one corner of the carriage. Karl sulked in the other. By the time they reached the House of the Black Spaniard, Beethoven was terribly ill. He burned with fever. He shook with chills. He was racked by a cough. The doctor said that he had pneumonia.

How good it was to be in his own bed, with Grandfather's picture looking down at him! To see from the window the cathedral spire and the rooftops of his beloved Vienna!

Karl went out to play billiards. Gerhard came running in to nurse the patient. He flitted so fast to do Beethoven's bidding that Beethoven changed his nickname to Ariel, the name of the fairy sprite in Shakespeare's play, *The Tempest*.

In January, 1827, Karl and his Uncle Ludwig had one last big quarrel. Then Karl went off to join his regiment. It was a pity that Beethoven did not live to see how his nephew changed. For Karl turned over a new leaf. A few years later he married. He went into business. He supported his family and became a respected citizen of Vienna.

Karl was not really bad. He just did not understand that his uncle was a genius, and that geniuses are different from other people. Their minds are full of great thoughts, and so they do not always notice what goes on around them, and this makes them behave strangely sometimes. Ordinary people have to make allowances for geniuses. Nobody had ever explained this to Karl.

When Karl left Vienna, his uncle was still ill in bed. But "Ariel" was there to help him through the long days that followed.

CHAPTER NINETEEN

Stormy Ending

BEETHOVEN recovered from pneumonia, but he did not get well. His worry over Karl had brought back his stomach trouble. Still, he hoped to compose his *Tenth Symphony*.

"I have never dreamed of writing for fame and honor," he told Ariel. "What weighs on my heart must come out, and that is why I have written."

His *Tenth Symphony* weighed on his heart. But he could not work at it. He knew he must go over his notes again and again, writing and rewriting, changing and improving, because that was the way he created his masterpieces. And he did not have the strength to do so.

Ariel brought to his bedside the presents people sent. From England came a welcome gift of money to pay the expenses of his illness.

[*177*]

From England, too, came a set of Handel's works, complete in forty big volumes. One at a time, Ariel lugged the heavy books to the bed, and leaned them against the wall, so that Beethoven could examine each one separately.

"I have long wanted them," Beethoven said, fingering the pages weakly. "Handel was the greatest, the most skilled composer who ever lived. I can still learn from him."

After this, he kept a volume of Handel on the table beside his bed, like a Bible. He said it was "a royal present," better than any other he had received.

Ariel brought Beethoven the dainties that people sent to tempt his appetite—champagne, puddings, out-of-season fruits, whatever he asked for. Doctors came to see him every day. When one did not cure him, he sent for another. But still he grew weaker.

The word spread that he was dying. Friends came to pay their last visit. Franz Schubert, a shy young man in spectacles, came for a few minutes. Beethoven liked the beautiful songs Schubert had composed, but was too ill to tell him so. Soon he was too ill to want to see anybody. Anton Schindler, a young man who had been his secretary for a time; his brother Johann; Stephan von Breuning, and of course

Ariel, continued to come. But Beethoven felt that he was best off when he was alone or with Ariel.

There was nothing more the doctors could do for him. A case of wine arrived, the last gift he was to receive.

"Pity, pity—too late," he murmured. Then he became unconscious.

Two days later, on the afternoon of March 26, 1827, there was a tremendous thunderstorm. Suddenly, a flash of lightning lit up the darkened room in which Beethoven lay unconscious, breathing heavily. A shattering clap of thunder followed. Beethoven opened his eyes. He lifted his right hand, clenched into a fist. He shook the fist, and heaved a great sigh. His hand fell back on the bedcover. He was dead.

He was buried on March 29th, at three o'clock in the afternoon. It was a day of beautiful sunshine. All day long, thousands of people crowded the streets surrounding the House of the Black Spaniard. Soldiers had to be called out to keep order, so large was the throng. The schools were closed to permit children, too, to pay their last respects to the great Beethoven.

The coffin was set in the square before the house. Beethoven's friends—poets, artists, and musicians—dressed all in black, with white roses attached to black crepe bands on their sleeves, gathered about it. There were so many friends that the coffin was completely hidden from the view of the crowd. A choir sang two of Beethoven's songs. Then the coffin was carried through the streets to the church. Though it was afternoon, and the sun was shining, the solemn procession that followed the coffin to the church carried blazing torches. The impressive funeral march from Beethoven's own piano sonata was played in Stephan von Breuning's house as the procession passed. It was as though a king were being buried.

In the Währing cemetery, another great crowd had collected. When the hearse halted at the gate, they listened with uncovered heads as an actor recited a poem written to honor the poet-musician, Beethoven. Then, to more strains of his own immortal music, Beethoven was laid to rest.

Because he wrote what he honestly thought and felt; because those thoughts and feelings were pure and noble; because he expressed them in music which has rarely been equaled in grandeur and tenderness, Ludwig van Beethoven reigns supreme in the world of music and in the hearts of music-lovers.

SOME RECORDINGS OF BEETHOVEN'S MUSIC

Bagatelles; Sonatas 8, 19, 20. For piano, played by Lily Kraus.
12" EDUCO 3006

Concerto No. 1 in C Major, Op. 15. For piano, played by Ania Dorfmann, and NBC Symphony Orchestra (Toscanini).
12" VICTOR LM–1039

Concerto No. 5 in E Flat Major, Op. 73 (Emperor). For piano, played by Clifford Curzon, and London Philharmonic Orchestra (Szell).
12" LONDON LLP114

Concerto in D Major, Op. 61. For violin, played by Distrakh, and Stockholm Festival Orchestra. (Ehrling).
12" ANGEL D35162

Egmont Overture; Symphony No. 1; Leonore No. 3. Played by Philharmonic Orchestra (Von Karajan). 12" ANGEL D35097

Minuets (12) for Redoutensaal; Romance. Played by Frankenland State Symphony Orchestra (Kloss). 12" LYRIC 45

Missa Solemnis in D Major, Op. 123. Soloists, Robert Shaw Chorale, NBC Symphony Orchestra (Toscanini).
2–12" VICTOR LM6013

Quartet No. 1 in F Major, Op. 18, No. 1; Quartet No. 2 in G Major, Op. 18, No. 2. Played by Budapest String Quartet.
12" COL. 4 ML–4576

Quartet No. 7 in F Major, Op. 59, No 1. (Rasumowsky). Played by Budapest String Quartet. 12" COL. 4 ML–4579

Rondo a Capriccio, Op. 129 (Rage over a Lost Penny): Sonatas No. 13 and No. 20 (piano). Played by Steurer.
12" URANIA 7033

Serenade in D Major, for flute, violin, viola, Op. 25; Trio, Op. 9. Played by Julius Baker, Joseph and Lilian Fuchs.
12" DECCA 9574

Sonata No. 14 in C Sharp Minor (Moonlight); Sonata No. 26 in E Flat Major (Les Adieux). Played by Rudolph Serkin (piano). 12" COL. 3 ML–4432

Sonata No. 21 in C Major, Op. 53 (Waldstein); Sonata No. 23 in F Minor, Op. 57 (Appassionata). Played by Gieseking (piano). 12" ANGEL D35024

Symphony, Op. 91 (Wellington's Victory); Viennese Dances: King Stephan Overture. Played by Paris Radio Symphony Orchestra (Leibowitz). 12" OCEANIC 34

Symphonies No. 1–9 Complete. Played by soloists, chorus, NBC Symphony Orchestra (Toscanini). 7–12" VICTOR M–6901

About the Author

HELEN L. KAUFMANN was born and brought up in New York, where she attended public school, Ethical Culture High School, and Barnard College. She is a violinist and has played in string quartets for many years. Indeed, music is her main interest, and most of her books are about music and musicians. Besides writing for magazines such as *Parents' Magazine* and *Musical America,* she has written many books, including *The Story of One Hundred Great Composers, The Little Guide to Music Appreciation, The Little Book of Music Anecdotes, The Little History of Music,* and the Signature Book, *The Story of Mozart.* She also has written the program notes for the Young People's Philharmonic concerts and now directs the music department of the American Committee for Emigré Scholars, Writers, and Artists.

About the Artist

FRITZ KREDEL was born in Michelstadt, Germany. He graduated from the Realgymnasium in Darmstadt and, after World War I, entered the Kunstgewerbeschule in Offenbach to study art under Professor Rudolf Koch. He then went to Florence, Italy, and studied for a year under Professor Victor Hammer, after which he returned to Offenbach and Professor Koch, and also worked as an instructor at the school. In 1938, he came to the United States. He became an American citizen and for two years was an art instructor at Cooper Union Art School. His illustrations for *Grimms' Fairy Tales, Pinocchio, Aesop's Fables,* and many other important books have earned him an enviable reputation as an artist, and have won several awards and citations, and the Medal of Honor from his native city of Michelstadt.

"Names That Made History"

Enid LaMonte Meadowcroft, *Supervising Editor*

1 Born in Bonn, Germany, December 16, 1770

2 Becomes deputy organist at Elector's Chapel in Bonn and starts to compose, 1782

3 Goes to Vienna to study with Haydn, 1792

4 Plays his own compositions at his first public concert in Vienna, 1795

10 Dies in Vienna after a long illness, March 26, 1827

9 Totally deaf, he conducts, but cannot hear, his "Ninth Symphon" and "Solemn Mass," 1824